THE ULTIMATE GUIDE TO SALARY NEGOTIATION

Jack van Minden

2000

For a complete list of Management Books 2000 titles
visit our web-site on http://www.mb2000.com

Based on the Dutch book "Op naar een hoger salaris" by Jack van Minden, published in the
Netherlands in 2007 by Business Contacts

This adapted UK edition first published in 2009 by Management Books 2000 Ltd
Forge House, Limes Road
Kemble, Cirencester
Gloucestershire, GL7 6AD, UK
Tel: 0044 (0) 1285 771441
Fax: 0044 (0) 1285 771055
Email: info@mb2000.com
Web: www.mb2000.com

British Library Cataloguing in Publication Data is available
ISBN 9781852525781

For Sosha – Later, she will understand why

Contents

Preface

Let's not beat about the bush: life is about money. Most of us weren't born in a golden cradle. Unfortunately, our parents had to melt down the silver spoon – and slave away for a living. And like them, unless we are lucky enough to win the lottery, we will have to do it ourselves, with our own hands and brains. It is up to us to make the most of our abilities – and that includes making sure we get paid as well as possible for them.

If, like the great majority of people, you have to earn your income with 'ordinary' work, wouldn't it be nice to increase your monthly salary with just 'a simple conversation'?

By the end of this book, you will know how to increase your salary rather easily. The saying 'you can't buy happiness' refers to the fact that there is more to life than a big income. However, no-one would deny that a bit of extra money (or even a lot of it) could positively increase the **quality** of your life.

Who is this book written for?

This book is indispensable for every working person who wants a raise, as well as newcomers to the job market. In addition, we include a section for women who do the same work as men but find they are paid less, and want to put this right!

Are you dealing with an employer who is offering you a ready-made remuneration package? If so, this book will give you help in assessing the real value of the package. Are your wages governed by a Union agreement? Are you a civil servant, subject to public sector wage controls? Never fear. You will find that there are many more financial possibilities than you – or your boss – might think!

Does your employer want to know what your ideas about compensation are? This book is your coach. Do you have to discuss a new salary on a yearly basis with your boss? You have knocked on the right door. This book is your basic toolkit.

The Ultimate Guide to Salary Negotiation is also useful for graduates and students trying to find their first job.

It's one thing to orientate yourself in the job market. It's something else to determine where the most attractive incomes are earned and how to get them. This is especially true for the large group of readers with little experience in the difficult and non-transparent terrain of salaries. Keep one eye on the job vacancies and the other eye on this book!

Checklists

This book has a number of checklists, practical lists of questions to prepare for a salary interview. You can check off discussion topics, set your boundaries and so on.

Finding your way on the web

At the end of each chapter we have included a number of websites that can help you even more on your way to a higher salary.

Exercises

You will find a number of exercises in this book. Do them. Fill in the lists. Write down your comments. 'Consume' this book! Because the more you practice and think about the next salary interview, the more confident you will be. That charisma will increase your chance for success!

Example sentences

In addition, we provide a range of model questions and answers – including phrases and sentences which will come in especially handy in your quest for a higher salary. If you expect to get yourself in an uncomfortable situation, then learn these sentences by heart during your preparation. That way your attack will not fail.

Advice for the reader

This book is packed full of advice and tips. Some are so important that we have set them in grey boxes like the one shown below.

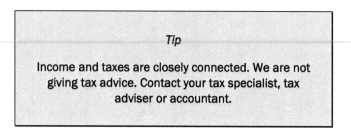

Tip

Income and taxes are closely connected. We are not giving tax advice. Contact your tax specialist, tax adviser or accountant.

Terminology

Professional jargon has been avoided whenever possible. The same applies to 'difficult' words. Our aim is to increase the readability of this book. (Have we succeeded? We would like to hear that from you, dear reader!).

When 'he' or 'him' are used in this book, you can read them as 'she' or 'her'. All male examples can be replaced by female ones (except in the chapter on women's pay!). For the sake of readability, we have opted to use the male gender throughout.

In this book, we use interchangeably a number of descriptions for the person you will be negotiating with – your 'opponent', 'the other party', 'your (future) boss', 'your (new) employer'. In all cases, the person we mean is the one who is responsible for all your sleepless nights and sweaty palms!

We do not promise you your own swimming pool (it's too cold anyway), a Ferrari (but there's always the speed limit) or a sea-going yacht. What we *can* promise is a higher salary – more cash, which you can do 'nice things' with!

Jack van Minden
Amsterdam, November 2008

1

Put your shoulder to the grindstone!

Nobody in the entire world takes better care of your interests than you do. If you don't stand up for yourself, who will? Your (future) boss? The personnel department? The trade union? The Conservative-Liberal-Labour-Party? The government? And if someone else looks after your needs, how motivated is he or she? And how single-minded?

You'll have to put in some effort if you want to raise your salary to a high or higher level. Leaving that to others rarely leads to satisfactory results.

They say that good preparation is half the work. Does that apply to your salary negotiation? Of course it does! These preparations will take quite a lot of time and will cost you quite a bit of energy but they determine three quarters of the success. (And that will especially pay off when your opponent hasn't done his homework.)

A skilful chat with your current or new employer is not enough to acquire a higher salary and interesting benefits. You need to have a number of skills to increase the chance of getting that raise. Do these methods guarantee success? Of course not. You will have to negotiate – and that's something you may not be used to – or give up the fight. That doesn't mean that when the next round of negotiations begins (in six months, next year, whenever) you have to be discouraged, downtrodden or submissive. Maybe it is not possible to increase your salary to a reasonable level due to financial setbacks within your organisation; keep on trying until the situation changes. We will also try to take away your fear of 'the talk'.

But let's start on an optimistic note – because it has been shown that there is always more in the financial pot than first appears – and always more than we're offered.

There's always more in the pot

You apply for a job that seems very interesting for the most part. Perhaps it is your first job; perhaps you want to change to a better position. The selection procedure is long and contains several interviews with the future employer and there is an intensive assessment. After ample time a decision has been made. The employer, in the form of your future boss or perhaps someone from Personnel, makes what seems to be a sweet offer. The crowning achievement for your hard work. You are just about to shout out your acceptance. Is that wise?

No matter how good the proposal is, there are always more options than you think. (If it is a proposal, the implication is that you have a choice!) If the future employer wants your services badly enough, you can give yourself time to think about it. It's usually no more than a couple of days! Do not sign the contract under any circumstances. Unless it's a galleon full of gold. Even if only a 1% increase can be negotiated, you will still have a better income! Now and in the future.

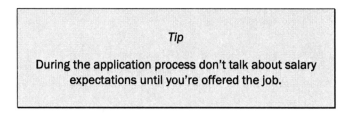

Tip

During the application process don't talk about salary expectations until you're offered the job.

The supply and demand game

Do you think that you have no 'power' as a job applicant? Or no rights? That may indeed *seem* to be the case, but in fact it is often not so. Are you one of the last few candidates left (perhaps the last one)? Has there been a lot of time invested in you? The employer wants to have a satisfactory outcome. You hold the trump card. Use it!

You represent a certain value. The organisation seems to want to take you on. They have had ample time to examine your qualities and skills and you seem to be the right person for the job. On the other hand, the organisation appeals to you. A 'price-tag' hangs around your neck, to be a bit disrespectful. The general price was set before the procedure even started. But before the exact price is set, both parties still have leeway.

The same applies when you already have a job. When the employer really wants to keep you, they'll make sure your (reasonable) wishes are met and pay the desired price. But first, you will have to decide for yourself if it's a good idea to ask for more. Take a critical look at the situation. What makes you think your estimate of your value is correct? (Refer to chapter 6.)

In the worst-case scenario, if you are not doing that great a job and they would be happy to see you leave, there is clearly not so much to negotiate. Of course, the labour market plays a big role here as well. Are you one of those sought-after specialists? Or were you trained in another century and is your trade little more than a tourist attraction? (Refer to the next chapter.)

Common questions about salary negotiations

Remember: the more an organisation is interested in you, the more it will be willing to pay the price. Your price. The trump card may be on your side!

You are not alone! Many of your colleagues share your insecurity when their own paycheque has to be negotiated. The most frequently asked questions are listed below. Some are from job applicants, some from shy co-workers.

- ◆ 'How much am I exactly worth to the organisation? And how do I find out what I'm worth in the labour market?'
- ◆ 'Next week I am meeting my director. How do I open the discussion?'
- ◆ 'How do I introduce the subject of money without spoiling the atmosphere or coming across like a hyena?'
- ◆ 'I haven't had a raise in three years. My boss doesn't want to speak about it, because – he says – I'm on too high a level as it is. How can I change his attitude?'
- ◆ 'What arguments should/can I use or not use?'
- ◆ 'What will happen if my negotiation attempt fails?'
- ◆ 'What can I do when my (present or future) boss or personnel officer flatly refuses to negotiate?'
- ◆ 'How do I react to the counter-offer if I want to reject it entirely?'
- ◆ 'How do I know if the employer's "last" offer is indeed his last offer or only a negotiation strategy?'
- ◆ 'Will threatening to quit work to my advantage?'
- ◆ 'How do I assess which is most advantageous: a small raise now, or profit-sharing starting next year?'
- ◆ 'The personnel manager explained that I will be placed under scale x in the remuneration system. That's not advantageous. What steps can I take?'
- ◆ 'I know that I have a little bit of leeway in the discussion. How do I find out how much it is?'
- ◆ 'What can be done when the employer's promises don't end up in the contract?'
- ◆ 'What concrete objectives should I have?'

- ◆ 'Am I prepared to take the consequences of a possible aborted meeting?'
- ◆ 'How is the relationship between performance and salary determined by management? Is there an objective way to measure this in every function?'
- ◆ 'I have been working for the same organisation for two years and am still at my starting salary. However, the tasks and responsibilities have grown immensely. How can I explain to my manager that the pay is lagging behind?'

Do you also wrestle with these issues? Do you recognise yourself in one or more of these questions? More than certain! Most of these questions will be answered in this book, so that you can confidently enter into the next discussion about your salary.

Change your mindset

Before you can become a good salary negotiator, you have to overcome yourself. What do we mean by that? Many people have difficulties telling their (current of future) boss what salary they want to earn. If you don't ask for an interesting raise, chances are that you're not going to get it. If you never ask, you'll never hear 'yes'. What do you have to lose? Even the smallest raise is pure profit compared with keeping your mouth shut.

A primary school arithmetic lesson: a raise will have positive consequences for years to come. Every subsequent salary increase will profit from this hike. As long as you stay with this employer, you will benefit, and you will almost certainly carry the increase forward to your next employer (who will base his offer on what you are earning in your current position).

Don't hesitate: every day is the right day to make a decision and to start 'talking'. A higher salary is within reach. However, you have to do something about it!

Fear of negotiating?

When you are afraid of damaging your image within the organisation, or your personal relationship with your boss, your choice is either not to bring up the topic or to get over the fear.

Think of what you have already negotiated in your life. Let's take a look. The summer vacation. You really want to take the family for an energetic mountaineering and restful nature-filled holiday in Switzerland. You want to make the trip by car. Your partner has other ideas: getting a great tan on a

Spanish beach and enjoying more than one paella. What will the holiday destination turn out to be? And how will you get there? After a difficult negotiation the compromise is to fly to Spain, spend one week enjoying the Sierra Nevada mountains and after that a one-week tanning regime – with a rental car.

Do we get the old TV repaired or is it 'cheaper' to buy a brand new one? You want to stay living in your inexpensive but small home while your partner wants to move to a larger, thus more expensive, home. You also have to come to agreements with your colleagues at work. Which tasks do you take on for a colleague who has been sick for a long time and which are assigned to someone else? Your office has to move to the third floor while you really enjoy the beautiful view from the twelfth floor! You talk to people higher up in the organisation. After a few discussions, you end up on the ninth floor.

When you have a closer look, you really do negotiate a lot. You have more experience at it than you thought. What are you afraid of then? What are you worried about?

This is the way not to do it!

You have the chance to say some very cynical and unfriendly things during a negotiation. Avoid them, even when they are on the tip of your tongue and you want to teach someone a lesson.

For instance:

♦ 'I have to have a life!'
♦ 'My wife and children will like that a lot.' (ironically)
♦ 'Do I look like I'm made of money?'
♦ 'You'll have to make a better offer than that.'
♦ 'You can't be serious!'
♦ 'There's no way I'm accepting that!'
♦ 'Is the decimal point is the right place?'(maliciously)

Nothing is ever won in a negotiation with these kinds of remarks. (You'll find appropriate sentences in chapter 8.)

> ### *Tip*
>
> **Don't let anyone confuse you. Remain resolute. It may take another year before you get the chance to talk about your salary again.**

Finding your way on the web

www.monster.co.uk
Tips about salaries and incomes

www.jobcentreplus.gov.uk
Jobsearch and benefits advice

2

The labour market

Writing about the labour market is difficult since there is not one labour market. There are many! Some 'perform' very well, others poorly. There are positions in the corporate world that pay better than similar positions in the government or institutions. It can also depend on where exactly you work or want to work. Furthermore, some sectors may be running well at the moment, while their future expectations are sober. The labour market is constantly in motion.

In this chapter, we will first look at stepping from one labour market to another. Then the hog cycle will be described. These pink animals can have quite an influence on your life – and we don't mean the price of bacon. Finally, we will discuss ten labour market trends.

From labour market to labour market

The labour market is an invisible 'marketplace' where vague economic forces continuously determine your value. You have to deal with a conflagration of economic forecasts, international developments and specific trends in a sector (for example technological breakthroughs, government subsidies or cuts).

Whether you want to or not, you are always part of a labour market and always influenced and ruled by it. You can choose to jump from one labour market to another. In many cases, that is a smart move. Two examples. You are a technician at a university. Everyone values your work. But you have noticed that over the past few years your employer has become stingier with the salaries. You have seen a fair number of colleagues leave. Some voluntarily, some with a bit of 'help'. Through a friend, you hear about a job opening with a successful medical equipment importer. This job pays more than twice your current salary. Do you remain loyal to the university? Or do you finally want to earn a good salary?

Second example. You are a teacher at a primary school. This job needs a lot of love for education and children, to make up for the ulcers, the heart complaints, and going into the red now and then. But dedication can wane.

And where can you go as a primary school teacher outside the field of education? You start looking, but all your interviews in related sectors, such as training, adult education and instructional film production lead to dead ends. In the meantime, you decide to take a marketing course (you never know if it will be useful). After four fruitless years of applying for jobs, an advertisement for a marketing staff member by a small family firm catches your eye. You get the job, which has nothing to do with marketing, but everything with selling. You are now a successful salesperson and laugh at your previous salary. (It goes without saying that a country should pay its professional educators well – the youth are the future – but that is a *political* problem!)

What can you learn from this? Make the change if you are sitting in the wrong labour market. You can probably flourish in more places than you think!

The point is to find out where precisely and in which labour market there are chances. However, do not concentrate only on the sectors that are doing well. You could possibly fit in well in an area where the employment possibilities are diminishing. Even in the most sombre years in the shipbuilding industry, there were personnel that did well financially. Despite the fact that the book industry has seen a drop in sales (and readership is down, not by you of course) many have found appealing, often well-paid, jobs. Books have to compete a lot with television, DVD and internet; even so, you cannot automatically conclude that every website owner 'has it made' and every bookseller is not doing well.

The hog cycle: peaks and troughs

The hog cycle is an old economic phenomenon. It means that when there is a shortage of hogs, the price of pork rises. Smart farmers notice this and start raising pigs. Unfortunately, there are so many who do this, that the supply of pork grows back to exceed the demand, leading to a fall in the price. After a while, the farmers do not want to raise their pigs for the small profits and switch (again in large numbers) to raising another kind of livestock. Thereby another shortage of pork begins again.

This 'farmer logic' is also found in the labour market. An example. For years, the media has been reporting on the great need for computer experts. Periodically there is a big demand for all kinds of specialists and sales representatives of continually more advanced hardware, software and internet applications. Many step over into the cyclical world of bits and bytes. There are special projects for unemployed academics to be quickly schooled as 'computer experts'. But this kind of 'farmer behaviour' gets penalised. The demand for employees in this market goes up and down (for many reasons) and that also applies to the salaries. Retrained academics find out that they have bet on the wrong horse (hog) for the second time.

Our message? Do not be tempted purely by the numbers. When 'everyone' has his eye on a given labour market, eventually there will be a change which is likely to make it less attractive.

Professions with a future?

Predicting what will happen in the labour market is risky because there are many (unseen) factors that throw a spanner in the works. Terrorism is bad for air travel and tourism. And your health. Financial scandals hinder the stock exchange. Even the most well set up academic research study cannot predict which direction the economy is heading in. Recession or boom, who can tell? Will the 'new Europeans' (from the former communist countries) move in greater numbers to the UK? Or will we have to deal with illegal Russian guest workers? How fast will automation destroy jobs? And how fast will it create them? Will a highly polluted environment create employment or will it push out 'dangerous' jobs? Or maybe both? Quite annoying: the future always throws a spanner in the works and our predictions never come true. There is naturally one fundamental question for you, 'How scarce are people with my training and professional background?'

Pay attention! Ten trends

Just like every other market, the labour market is in constant motion. There are a number of current trends that you need to know about. We list below ten trends which you should be aware of in mapping out your salary expectations.

1 Knowledge specialisation and knowledge obsolescence

We are living in an era where considerable numbers of specialists specialise in specialisations that encompass an increasingly smaller field. There is a demand for these super-specialists – especially when they know how to sell their field of expertise! Nowadays there is an incredible amount researched, developed, discussed and published in every field of expertise. It seems that there is only one way to keep one's head above the endless waves of information: digging infinitely deep into a specialisation of a specialisation. In this way, the complete picture can be kept in view, since the super-specialist only has to deal with a limited number of collegial experts and just a few highly specialised professional journals.

'The one who publishes gets tenure'. Specialists who write get recognition, which increases their market value. (That does not say anything about the quality of their work.) No one has ever been worse off from 'personal-pr'! Besides that, magazine publishers feel the hot breath of the next edition breathing down their necks: authors need to be approached to make sure the issue is full of news and tips. The result of all of this is that today's knowledge is quickly obsolete. Anyone who hasn't practiced his profession for a number of years and hasn't kept up with the developments will notice to his greatest shock that he has fallen hopelessly behind!

2 Creativity

'The one who publishes gets tenure'. However, the world bows to the creative. People with (lasting) creative ideas will do well in every labour market – and they can make demands.

Tip

Even when you have a great job, make sure others notice you. Publish an article regularly in your trade journals or popular magazines, or stay in the news in another way, for example with interviews or talking at congresses or meetings. Getting your name across will increase your market value in the long run.

---

3 Entrepreneurial spirit

Nowadays many businesses are more interested in leaders who are born entrepreneurs than in pure managers. There is an increasing demand for 'intrapreneurs': enterprising managers who have a free hand in the organisation/division/department) to lead it as an entrepreneur. Someone willing to take initiative. That means that you have to be a different kind of manager. During your salary negotiations, mention the initiatives that you have taken or will soon take.

4 Flexibility

Even without natural resources, the Japanese economy is a success thanks to the flexibility of its workers. These loyal employees are expected, in fact told, to take on other tasks when the economical situation asks for it. A bookkeeper is retrained as a sales manager, a designer as a marketing manager, a production assistant as a receptionist. Employees are parachuted into positions that need their energy. This management philosophy offers advantages to both parties. The organisations can react more effectively and quicker to changes without having to lay off employees or recruit, select and train new ones. The personnel are continually challenged and can keep learning new skills.

5 People are key

Any organisation is only as good as its people. The quality, energy and motivation of the employees make or break it. It is not surprising that more and more attention is being paid to the careful selection of new personnel, training, career policies, salaries and so on. This is the hunting ground of HRM, human resources management.

6 Mobility of 'toppers'

Large organisations expect top managers to be prepared to move from one location to another one, from country A to country B. Managers are expected to be mobile. At the same time, more and more managers are leaving their companies voluntarily to look for better opportunities. Furthermore, it is evident that top managers have an ever shorter lifespan within their organisations. Just like a football trainer, when business results are poor, the manager must leave. It is expected that in turbulent times we will have to pick up the speed of the musical chairs.

7 Decreasing loyalty

The loyalty of many employees lies closer to the profession than to the employer. When hiring and firing employees is made easy everywhere – a necessity with the ever-increasing international competition and globalisation – we can expect loyalty to go down even more.

> **Tip**
>
> Developing and maintaining a professional network is important. You will not only profit in your current function (you 'hear about things'), but you will also broaden your personal horizons. When necessary, you can get information from your network about vacancies, salaries, etc.

8 New forms of remuneration

Remuneration is not only about the gross salary (next chapter). It is expected that forms of remuneration will become more flexible. (Refer to the cafeteria plan in Chapter 4.) Performance-based rewards will most likely gain interest – especially in functions where effort, and above all, results can be measured. A shift from a high fixed salary to a smaller fixed monthly payment with performance-related 'extras' and profit-sharing can be expected. More often than not, you will have to use a calculator to figure out what your monthly income is.

Some experts believe that professionals will look for more financial security. That means building up and maintaining their capital by acquiring shares in the business, options, extensive pension plans and the like.

9 Internationalisation/globalisation

The fact that the world is becoming one village is a dream come true for some and a nightmare for others. A mutual international dependency has emerged that continues to grow, bringing advantages and disadvantages. Economic downfalls in one country will be felt more quickly in another. Sooner or later, that will also translate to more uncertainty in your job. Big international mergers between companies or break-ups can put your own position in danger, sooner than you think possible.

10 Future shortages

Demographers predict a large labour shortage.

Will people from the growing European Union therefore pack up their bags more often and move to countries with higher gross salaries and a milder financial climate? An example. An average senior sales manager in the IT in the Netherlands earns €61,000. Including bonuses, the total remuneration comes to €95,000. His German colleague earns €69,000 and with his year-end bonus, his earnings total € 115,000. That is a gross difference of €20,000. Furthermore, the German income tax is considerably lower. (And housing is often less expensive.)

Finding your way on the web

www.nomisweb.co.uk
Labour market information

www.statistics.gov.uk/STATBASE/Product.asp?vlink=550
Labour market statistics

www.prospects.ac.uk/cms/ShowPage/Home_page/Labour_market_information/plefeXak
Labour market information for graduates

3

What do you think you're worth?

Who doesn't want to know the answer to: 'What am I really worth?' and 'How can I find that out?' In this chapter, our discussion will include how to gather information over your own 'market value'. Armed with the correct knowledge, this will allow you to start the negotiations on the right foot and ultimately fill your own treasure chest. We will also test your memory and determine what your personal needs are besides money. While the chance to own your own swimming pool may mean a lot to you, it may mean that you need to work so hard that there is no time left for a refreshing relaxing swim!

Over and underpaid?

Harvey Mackay, author of *Swim With the Sharks Without Being Eaten Alive* has a theory about salary levels which might strike a chord. You don't need to agree, but it is food for thought. Mackay suggests that as people start their first job, they are always massively overpaid bearing in mind their total lack of experience and their need for training. However, within a few years, as they become experienced and pick up training, and their pay fails to rise accordingly, they then become significantly *under*paid. They remain in this state for up to 20 years unless and until they slip into the management stratum, at which point they then become *over*paid again! The trick, he says, is to make the middle period (the period when you are underpaid) as short as possible – by picking the right time, once you have got your qualifications and basic experience, to seek promotion or leave for a new job.

Do you have a stingy boss?

How salary-conscious are you? A memory exercise

Do you have any idea about your monthly income? From memory, write down in the table below what your gross annual income is, including bonuses, benefits and social security payments and what that means for the net income. Base it on this year or last year, so that it gives the most accurate representation of your situation.

Can you fill in the following table without looking at your labour contract and/or monthly salary statement?

Part of income	Gross (year)	Net (year)
Salary		
Commission		
Company car		
Travel costs		
Business expenses		
Health insurance benefits		
Pension contributions		
Annual bonus		
Profit sharing		
Telephone costs (fixed/mobile)		
Other		
Total		

Question 1. Is your present gross-income better or worse than you expected? And what about the calculated net income?

Question 2. Compare the results of your chart with the actual terms of your employment contract. How well informed are you about how much your job 'pays'?

Resources and summaries

Most people in the business world – regardless of their training, occupation, function and salary level – have little insight into their 'market value'. That can create problems for salary negotiations! Civil servants have it easier. The government publishes yearly salary summaries for its employees. However, there are several sources of information which you can consult without even getting out of your armchair, while there are others where you will need to do some investigation to get 'fresh' information. We list below the most important information resources available.

Internet

The internet is without a doubt the most consulted source of salary scales. Well-known income indicators and salary guidelines are found on a variety of websites. The government also makes its salary scales available on the net. Refer to the websites noted at the end of this and other chapters as well.

Job advertisements in daily and weekly newspapers

Job advertisements can give a useful indication of the going rate for particular types of job. However, note that advertisements for more senior jobs often do not specify the salaries offered; they may state a broad range, or a minimum rate ('salary in excess of...'), may state 'salary dependent on experience', or may rely on bland generalisations such as 'Excellent rewards' with 'pension benefits'.

Industry and professional associations

Certain associations (accountants, roofers, engineers, psychologists, retail workers, the automotive industry, etc.) sometimes publish salary reviews in members' newsletters or magazines.

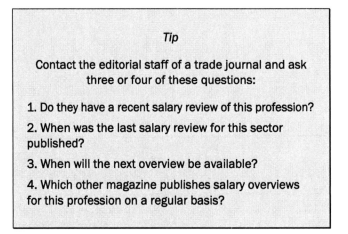

Tip

Contact the editorial staff of a trade journal and ask three or four of these questions:

1. Do they have a recent salary review of this profession?

2. When was the last salary review for this sector published?

3. When will the next overview be available?

4. Which other magazine publishes salary overviews for this profession on a regular basis?

Office for National Statistics

The ONS publishes general salary and earnings data (see also the previous chapter).

Network

Consult your network of colleagues, friends, acquaintances and family members. Unfortunately, 'salary' is still not an acceptable topic of conversation at receptions, parties or with company. At least when it's your own salary.... Try asking a colleague about his or her payslip!

Jobcentre Plus

Jobcentre Plus has its own sources, but it is not clear how accurate they are. This can be a source of information for middle management positions but definitely not for upper management.

The media

Data and indications regularly appear in the media. Most often, it is the research or investigation of an enthusiastic or frustrated journalist or even more often a rewritten press release from a specialised agency. The most well known are Hay, Towers Perrin, Mercer and Watson Wyatt. Their figures come from annual research of the business world. Unfortunately, their reports are not free of charge or even cheap. Most of us will have to make do with what filters through in the press, or make use of informal contacts.

Government and business

Concrete salary information is also available from governmental organisations and large companies that have published labour agreements, job profiles and salary scales.

Recruitment and selection agencies/headhunters

Contacting so-called 'headhunters' will also produce fairly concrete information. These advisers know what their clients want to pay and can therefore act as a fairly reliable source of information. These intermediaries must always give you a salary indication for a particular job. How else do you know if it is worth considering? (And that applies to your competitors as well.)

These agencies will give you a ballpark figure. For instance, their clients will be prepared to offer between £45,000 and £55,000 for the position.

Often there is also a 'plus-plus' mentioned. You will find out what this cryptic slogan means when you get down to negotiations. While you won't get accurate information, you will be able to determine if the job is financially interesting for you.

Keep in mind that the intermediary makes money out of you (indirectly). That means that they will be more than willing to help you and that your questions about income will be well answered. When the headhunter has invested time in you and has presented you as a candidate, he will certainly appreciate it – let's explain it that way – when your placement goes ahead. If you pull out of the negotiation process, that will cost the headhunter time. And time is money.

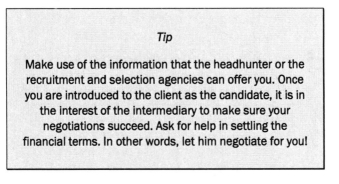

Tip

Make use of the information that the headhunter or the recruitment and selection agencies can offer you. Once you are introduced to the client as the candidate, it is in the interest of the intermediary to make sure your negotiations succeed. Ask for help in settling the financial terms. In other words, let him negotiate for you!

Employer

We shouldn't forget the (potential) employer that may present a salary indication during the job interview, salary negotiations, assessment and/or performance interview. An 'investigative' job interview may also produce valuable information.

Corridors and gossip

At congresses, professional meetings and in the pub you hear interesting things. Sometimes honest salary information, but mostly exaggerated and/or untrue. You are a one-person jury. However, it can still pay to keep your ears open.

College or campus recruitment

This form of orientation applies to a select group of (future) job hunters: postgraduate, to a lesser degree, undergraduate students. Employers are looking for those rare flowers, at an early stage, and hope to pluck them before their competitors do.

Recruiters will often visit campuses to make presentations. After a talk, PowerPoint and sweets, companies are offered the chance to meet (promising) graduates. Whilst these meetings are often poorly attended they can provide a useful source of information if the right questions are asked.

Job fairs

Job fairs are a trusted phenomenon in labour land. Their popularity goes up and down with the flow of the economy. There are general and specific fairs, the latter focusing on one specific type of business such as ICT. This is often an efficient way for an organisation to present itself and quickly make a lot of contacts. Fair visitors with real interest are often disappointed by the brief superficial contact.

Don't let this scare you off. Why should less than perfect information deter you from the earliest start of a salary negotiation?

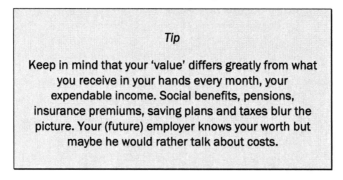

Tip

Keep in mind that your 'value' differs greatly from what you receive in your hands every month, your expendable income. Social benefits, pensions, insurance premiums, saving plans and taxes blur the picture. Your (future) employer knows your worth but maybe he would rather talk about costs.

In short, there are many sources available to gauge your market value. However, a few words of warning are appropriate:

♦ The stated sources often work with general or broad-based indicators, which may not necessarily reflect rates in specific areas or business subsectors.

♦ There are big differences between the financial rewards offered by government, non-profit organisations and business. By the same token there are also huge differences between financial rewards offered by large bureaucratic commercial organisations and smaller businesses.

♦ Some sectors offer more possibilities than others, just as there will be more demand for some types of professional than for others.

♦ Age, training and experience all play a role in the ultimate price tag. Every person is unique.
♦ There are sometimes regional differences. A strong employer in an 'isolated' region, with few competitive employment opportunities will sometimes have a certain hold on the local labour market. (Would you like to move from a traffic-free rural location to a large city? Your increased salary may well be eaten up by higher housing costs.)

Tip

An excellent negotiation argument is to determine your 'replacement value'. If you leave your employer, a successor will have to be recruited, selected and trained. That means weeks, if not months, of limited productivity. The total costs to the employer may well exceed £10,000, or more. That may be rather a large amount compared with the modest raise you are after.

Keep earning more

In public sector organisations, and in certain other more bureaucratic organisations, there is often a fixed salary scale including standard periodic pay raises for personnel. Employees and job applicants know beforehand what their future financial expectations might be. The route is easily predicted as long as there are no accidents along the way.

For some people it is nice to know precisely what they will be earning in four or fifteen years – and which carefully described tasks go with that. Others want more excitement and uncertainty in their lives. Probably they like to take a gamble: a relatively risky future, but a better chance for earning more. How do you see yourself?

Even when you are already in or will enter a situation with fixed salaries, it doesn't mean you have to take what you're handed. You still have a number of options:

1. How many people are available inside and outside the organisation for your chosen function? When there is a scarcity the world is your oyster.

Research will have to determine how much the laws of supply and demand will benefit you.

2. What are the benefits like? How much leeway do the rules allow? If there are no fixed agreements, then you have a wide-open playing field.

3. What is your career plan? Which direction have you set for yourself? What can the organisation offer you? Maybe you can negotiate an accelerated career path within the organisation (when appropriate).

4. If the organisation has periodic raises in addition to the position scales, your experience may work to your benefit so that you move up the pay ladder.

What is important to you? An exercise

What motivates you? Which personal needs do you want your career or following job(s) to fulfil? With the help of the following list, you can easily determine what they are – and naturally, you can philosophise about it. When you are done, it is a good idea to talk to others about it. It's possible that they will help you sharpen your ideas even more.

Question 1. Check off which personal needs you want to have met in your next career move.

Question 2. Check off which personal needs are the least important to you in your next career move.

Question 3. We can assume that you have a few problems with your current job. Perhaps they are not serious but more vague feelings. Check off which three problems you may be having in your current employment.

	Question 1	Question 2	Question 3
High salary			
High bonus/profit sharing			
Status			
Prestige			
Lots of friends			
Good relationship with colleagues			
Good relationship with managers			
Work close to home			
Make use of my expertise			
Recognition of my expertise			
Power			
Independence			
Challenge			
Recreation possibilities			
Training and education possibilities			
Keeping up with the latest developments			
Promotion possibilities			
Hold a management position			
Lots of free time			
Time for the family			
Security			
Worry-free work			
Cultural possibilities			
Prominent position in the organisation			
Prominent position in the industry /profession			
A lot of responsibility			

It goes without saying that the above list can be added to. Write down which personal needs you still have. Name as many as you want.

	Question 1	Question 2	Question 3
a			
b			
c			
d			
e			
f			
g			

Job descriptions

Many large companies and government organisations describe their positions in profiles or standardised job descriptions. There is a 'price-tag' associated with the profile.

We are continually surprised that so many smaller organisations – and definitely not just mediocre firms – haven't got job descriptions for advertised job vacancies. Why not? No time! How can job applicants be properly screened when their capacities, skills, competencies, qualities cannot be compared with the position? And the profile is not only useful in recruitment – it is also an essential reference in the process of ongoing performance appraisal (including the annual review).

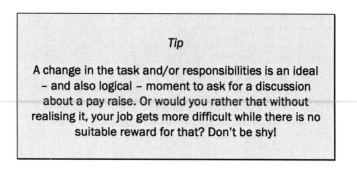

Tip

A change in the task and/or responsibilities is an ideal – and also logical – moment to ask for a discussion about a pay raise. Or would you rather that without realising it, your job gets more difficult while there is no suitable reward for that? Don't be shy!

The Hay system

International consultancy agencies such as Towers Perrin, Hay, Mercer and Watson Wyatt carry out research for companies on a yearly basis to determine the 'content' and salaries of positions objectively. Their reports are important instruments for personnel managers. They learn what the competition pays for comparable positions – and can adjust their salaries to these levels if necessary.

Perhaps the best-known method of job evaluation is the Hay system devised and copyrighted by consultant Ned Hay in 1948. Under this system each job is analysed in terms of three different types of skill requirement (know-how, problem-solving, and accountability), with points being allocated for each level. The aggregate point-score for the job then determines its value range, having reference to objectively researched market rates.

This kind of system offers the employer a number of advantages:

◆ Objectivity
◆ Informed discussion regarding job values
◆ Smoother negotiation of salaries (which are standardised)

What does an employee have to pay attention to when confronted with 'Hay', or similar systems?

1. The system is a good attempt to compare positions objectively. However, assessment still requires people's input. For instance, who decides the difference between two levels know-how applicable under the Hay system?
2. Each position carries a prescribed salary range (a bandwidth), which obviously limits your ability to negotiate outside the range.
3. The employee can be silenced because the personnel manager hides too easily behind 'the system'. And the direct 'boss' or supervisor? They point back to the Personnel department.

Finding your way on the web

www.thesalaryindicator.co.uk
To calculate net pay

www.hmrc.gov.uk/nmw
National minimum wage

www.wageindicator.org
www.payscale.com/resources.aspx?nc=lp_calculator_united kingdom01
www.reed.co.uk/CareerTools/SalaryCalculator.aspx
Payscale guidelines

4

Your salary breakdown

You need to decide what you want from your (future) employer, including any benefits you are seeking. Three weeks per year sailing with the company's fully manned pleasure yacht, harboured in the Bahamas? (Not a bad plan!) However, if you have any ideas that are closer to home, keep in mind that the boys at the HMRC will want to 'sail' along with you. As far as the taxman is concerned: 'Dancing is fun for two.'

This chapter deals with creative rewards, which the government tax collectors hate so much, but where there is still a bit of 'leeway' – even though it is getting less all the time. We would like you to pay attention to a number of noteworthy points. First, think long and deep about your most important goal: the desired (or dreamed) gross salary. (Some people are embarrassed to talk about something as common as salary. They would rather talk about the 'remuneration package'. You can naturally call it that as well.) It is your task to demonstrate to your (future) employer that you are worth that (high) salary. Which arguments are you going to throw into the arena? Why those ones?

After establishing your gross salary, you will need to focus on the additional benefits. In this chapter you will find a long checklist of benefits and other forms of compensation that you can deposit in front of your boss. You will be asking for quite a bit if you literally follow this checklist. We advise you to show a bit of reserve! A number of points on your wish list will be explained in more detail. But first, we offer a bit of background information about the salary hunting grounds.

The remuneration package

Your remuneration package is often broken down into two categories, salary and benefits. Primary is the gross salary, secondary is all the other forms of benefits. Think about the company car, pension benefits, health insurance and so on. Some go even further with tertiary and quaternary compensation. Tertiary is the (paid) parking place in the parking garage at your company.

With quaternary, you might want to think about the WC freshener in the board of directors' loo.

The cafeteria plan

The cafeteria plan is a form of flexible rewards. It has nothing to do with toasted sandwiches, chips curries and chowders or other fast food that eagerly lays waiting in the company restaurant for hungry clients. The name comes from the freedom, within legal boundaries, that employees are allowed to choose from their financial menu (= total remuneration package). High salary and few vacation days? Or perhaps the other way around? Reserving a portion of the salary to buy shares or stock options in the company every year? That's sometimes possible too. An extra high or accelerated pension plan? That can be discussed.

What is nice about the cafeteria plan is that it is financially attractive to both employers and employees, since there are a number of tax-related shifts and, in practice, productivity goes up. A young employee can 'buy' days off from his employee; an older employee may want to work more, in order to build up a bigger pension.

The employer with a cafeteria system usually uses a point or money system. Points can be collected and spent at one's own discretion on:

♦ salary (higher/lower);
♦ workdays/overtime (more/less);
♦ length of the workday (shorter/longer);
♦ insurance (supplementary, or fewer policy conditions);
♦ pension (higher/lower);
♦ early retirement (via deferred salary leave plan);
♦ holidays/free days (more/less);
♦ study (leave) days.

This flexible system is not used very often, but the expectation is that its popularity will increase. As long as your organisation does not have an 'official' cafeteria plan, you can take the initiative and together with the boss 'play' with a number of employment conditions (read: remuneration).

> **Tip**
>
> The primary compensation is the gross salary. No matter how attractive and fantastic all benefits are, always begin the negotiation about the salary that you need to pay the baker and the bank. Moreover, that will probably not be possible with the 'extra' benefits or the do-it-yourself-dental-drill-kit that the company provides free of charge.

What do you want to get?

Before you start 'talking', you need to make a plan: which points do you want to negotiate? Are you a sporty kind of character who rides a motorcycle, surfs the internet, plays chess, does crosswords and even walks to the car? Does the boss have to finance your hobbies and leisure activities? Is that reasonable? Is that what you really want to get out of it?

Determine what your minimum salary must be. (Refer to the scheme below.) What is the minimum gross income that is acceptable for you? In the previous chapter, there were a number of sources you can refer to in determining your 'market value'.

It is also handy to make a critical analysis of the organisation itself. Gather as much information possible about your company. Request the annual report, for instance by the company's website or via the Chamber of Commerce. What is the company's market position? Is there talk of a downfall or growth, what is happening with the turnover? (A company that is doing well can obviously do more than an ailing company.)

Formulate your 'big' goals, aided by the checklist below. What do you want to reach in the **short term** and what in the **long term**? The results of this exercise will end up on the negotiation table!

	Salary growth	
	Short term (<1 year)	Long term (>1 year)
Desired salary (gross)		
after 1 year		
after 2 years		
after 3 years		
Your minimum salary		
after 1 year		
after 2 years		
after 3 years		
Maximum attainable salary, if known (for example via advertisements or head-hunters)		
Which pay scale/how many years of service		
Split salary via foreign subsidiaries?		

Which scale?

Once the company has set your scale, then it's game over, so it appears. However, you don't need to give up immediately or accept the offered salary right away. Why are they offering that scale in particular? Make a point of discussing this.

Your first step: get scaled in at a higher level. This is not a pipe dream. When you don't take the initiative, your counterpart won't bring it up!

Besides the freedom employers enjoy to choose a certain scale, there are also possibilities to grant all kinds of privileges and incentives – even in those rigid governmental organisations. For instance, there are the 'signing bonuses' and similar bonuses. Government employers grant these to civil servants as a shield; they are a way of competing against the often better-paid corporate jobs. A top civil servant can also demand a company car. (At the very top there is a car and driver.) If an employer really wants to get a hold of someone, then they will play with the scale in order to offer a favourable entry salary.

Supporting the arguments!

As already mentioned: make your salary wishes more credible by supporting them with arguments. Indicate in the following list, which logical arguments apply to you. Consider the list carefully and write them down in order of strength.

We have already provided a few examples in italics. Do you have limited or no work experience? Fill these lists in anyway. Since you need arguments to justify a higher salary!

NB: Naturally, these same arguments can also be used at the job interview. You could be chosen based on these strong points.

Besides that, you will often be asked what you want to earn. Don't give too specific an answer since you can be pinned down. Are there more responsibilities in the future position than in your present one? Make sure that it is clear that you want to get ahead financially. Moreover, you want the difficulty of the function to be reflected in the financial rewards. Is there a job profile available? Then you can analyse it point by point if the offered salary matches with your work experience and responsibilities.

Write down the **concrete arguments** why you think you are worth the salary you want to get. Name as many that apply for this job as possible. The examples printed in italics have been picked at random.

Give as many concrete arguments as you can based on your **work experience**. (For instance, think about your successful projects.)

1.	*Worked three years in Nigeria under extremely primitive conditions. (Would they believe that?)*
2.	
3.	
4.	
5.	
6.	
7.	
8.	
9.	
10.	

Give as many examples of your skills and capacities as you can.

1.	*Very good at delegating, which has been shown at every assessment so far. Therefore, my productivity is very high. (How high? Compared with what?)*
2.	
3.	
4.	
5.	
6.	
7.	
8.	
9.	
10.	

Give as much evidence as you can regarding education, training courses and seminars you have attended (and completed).

1.	*Bachelor of Economics with a course in French (fluent?) and an MBA from Henley Management College.*
2.	
3.	
4.	
5.	
6.	
7.	
8.	
9.	
10.	

Give as many examples as you can of relevant activities outside your work.

1.	*Chairperson of the Ace tennis club and secretary of the Amora school board. ("So I have a lot of contacts.")*
2.	
3.	
4.	
5.	
6.	
7.	
8.	
9.	
10.	

Tip

When you hear before or during the negotiations that your salary will grow in the coming years, find out from the employer what kind of 'growth' they mean. Is it the same as you have in mind? Try to get the basis for the intended raises written into the contract.

Checklist of benefits

Earlier in the book, we argued that the most important thing you must fight for is the size of your salary. This is what you have to live off. However, don't get too fixed on this one point. Many benefits may suit your fancy. A salary that you think is (too) low may be compensated with attractive 'extras'.

There is an alphabet of possibilities for a better life: automobile, back massages, pension, and so on. The following list is a fairly complete list of benefits.

Explanation

1. This checklist *systematically* maps out the many 'extra' rewards available.
2. Select the ones that are most important to you and which you want to bring to the negotiation table. Limit the number and type of benefits to ones that (can) correspond with your job's level and status.
3. Choose one or two that you can easily surrender during negotiations. For example, imagine that you want to go to an important congress to keep your professional knowledge up to date. If the company's training allowance is very generous, surrender this 'trading card' during the negotiations providing that your *other* wishes are met.
4. Make sure that for each condition, it is clear exactly what you want. For instance if you want a company car, specify the minimum lease price (say, £800 per month) or a certain brand and model. In the case of moving costs, be sure that it is agreed that the costs are related to the position, and that they are compensated completely and with no maximum limit. Extra costs, for example redecorating, reupholstering and drapes may be compensated to a maximum of, say, £5,000. When you document what's been agreed upon, you will avoid future disappointments. And the employer will too.
5. Prioritise your wishes from absolutely necessary (first place) to 'tradable' (last place).
6. What do you negotiate first? Put the 'most expensive' and/or the ones that you think will take the most effort to get at the top of your list. The simpler points will be more easily accepted when both parties are tired out from the struggle and/or in a 'yes mood'.

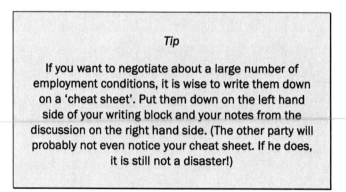

Tip

If you want to negotiate about a large number of employment conditions, it is wise to write them down on a 'cheat sheet'. Put them down on the left hand side of your writing block and your notes from the discussion on the right hand side. (The other party will probably not even notice your cheat sheet. If he does, it is still not a disaster!)

Checklist

Concrete wishes, and possible exceptions

1. Company car
♦ Which category/brand/class?
♦ What kind of fuel?
♦ Maximum mileage?
♦ Available budget?
♦ Free choice within budget?
♦ Your own contribution?
♦ Can you buy the car from the leasing agency at the end of the contract?
♦ If yes, at a fixed price? Or at market value?

2. Business expenses
♦ Dependent on the kind of position, how much time 'outside' the office and receiving guests at home.
♦ NB: Watch out for tax implications!

3. Travel expenses
♦ Commuting distance?
♦ Public transport/own car?
♦ Train pass? (First/second class?)
♦ NB: Watch out for fiscal limitations!

4. Telephone costs
♦ Monthly amount? (Fixed or variable?)
♦ Fixed line/mobile/DSL?

5. Company-paid health insurance
♦ Supplementary insurance?
♦ Which percentage paid by employer?
♦ Dental work?

6. Other insurance
♦ Life insurance?
♦ Risk/accident insurance?
♦ Liability insurance?
♦ Legal assistance?

7. Loans
♦ Maximum permitted amount?
♦ Interest rates?
♦ Term?
♦ Monthly payments?
♦ Other (soft) conditions?

8. Company savings plans
♦ Salary savings scheme?
♦ Deferred salary scheme?
♦ Stock option plan?
♦ How many shares per year?
♦ Contribution or free?
♦ Regular shares or special 'personnel shares'?
♦ Yearly growth (including dividends and splits)?
♦ Sale of shares, at which price and under which conditions (lock-up period)?

9. Pension
♦ Commencement date for participation?
♦ Which costs?
♦ Employer's contribution?
♦ Employee's contribution?
♦ Non-transferable pension rights?

10. Profit-sharing/bonus
♦ What is the company's policy?
♦ Is it based on the company's total results?
♦ Based on individual performance?
♦ Or both?
♦ Fixed remuneration?
♦ Fixed percentage of income? Variable?

11. Commission
♦ Which percentage?
♦ Incremental scale?
♦ Special provisions for exceptional actions/periods/products/services?

12. Overtime
♦ Compensation policy (time and/or money)

13. Flexible working hours
♦ Telework?

14. Training
♦ Which and when?
♦ Who pays for which costs (tuition, books, materials, exams, travel costs etc.)?
♦ Any other conditions?
♦ NB. Watch out for a penalty for early resignation

15. Conferences/seminars/study trips?
♦ Which and where?
♦ Under which conditions?

16. Golden parachute and outplacement
♦ Buy out premium/golden parachute (amount)?
♦ Outplacement agency (maximum amount)?

17. Holidays
♦ Number of mandatory days?
♦ Is there an incremental scale?
♦ Extra unpaid leave of absence?
♦ Extra paid leave of absence?

18. Sabbatical period (longer periods of unpaid (study) leave, or tied to a deferred salary leave plan)

19. Unpaid leave

20. Use of a company vacation home (yacht?)

21. Moving expenses
♦ How much is the compensation?
♦ Decorating costs?

22. Purchase/sale own home

23. Compensation for special situations

24. Discounts on company products/services

25. Payment in kind
- NB: How does the tax department regard this?

26. Credit card(s)
- Payment of membership fees?
- Spending limit?

27. Membership fees for professional organisations

28. Professional journals
- Which?
- What kind of budget is available?
- Sent to your home?

29. Membership fees for other organisations (service club, golf club, country club)

30. Fitness club membership/fees

31. Home computer and accessories

32. Company parking place

33. Childcare (day care)
- Employer's contribution?

34. Tax advice

35. Loyalty bonus

36. Other employment conditions

Again: you're not meant to take *all* these points into your negotiations. However, as you see, there are many possibilities and we advise you to cash in on a few of these.

> **Tip**
>
> A warning: any untaxed compensation is not protected
> by any form of social security and does not count
> towards your pension. That means that you have to
> make a choice between a higher gross income now
> and the possibility of a lower payment (health
> payments, unemployment benefits, etc.) later.

As you know, your friends in the tax department are more than happy to profit from your wealth. Whether it is correct or not, they will ask you to give up a large part of it. Many of the above benefits are taxable and will need to be declared in the P11D form filed by your employer with HMRC. For advice on the tax implications of employment benefits see www.hmrc.gov.uk/paye/exb-intro-basics.htm.

Information regarding the checklist

Company cars

A company car is the most well known secondary employment benefit and is on many employment contracts. Pay attention to the details. What kind (make) of car is it? What kind of budget is available? Do you have a choice as long as you stay within the guidelines? What is the maximum annual mileage that the lease price is based on? Is it allowable to get a better car by paying extra?

Furthermore, it is sometimes more interesting tax-wise to take out a loan for a car by your (future) employer. You pay it off based on the legal maximum per mile that you are fiscally allowed to. Maybe you and your boss find it difficult to figure out the exact mileage. A new company car is usually less expensive than the (financial) worries of a motorised goldmine.

What are the advantages of a leased car for both parties?

Employee	Employer
♦ Reliable transportation	♦ Nice incentive for employee (loyalty)
♦ Always a new car	♦ Lower tax basis
♦ Replacement car in the event of repairs or accident	♦ Capital is not tied up
♦ No personal investment	♦ Limited administration (no declarations or 'travel bills')
♦ Can also use it during vacations and weekends.	♦ No maintenance costs

Work out for your boss that a company car is not expensive when you already receive compensation for commuting and for business trips. To lessen the pain you can offer to pay a small portion of the monthly lease costs yourself (tax deductible!) It goes without saying that you make sure you get your salary raise first, so that you actually reward yourself.

The HMRC allows you do to do what your boss wants you to do: keep your (lease) car clean. (Your vehicle is also an advertisement for the employer – a dirty car stands for a dirty company in the eyes of some customers.) When your employer pays you for cleaning, you won't hear anything from the tax department. A £10 wash and wax is reasonable; this is the amount it would cost every week at a carwash or if you got out the sponge and soap yourself.

Many people negotiate blue in the face to get a leased car. However, there are also people that *don't* want a car. They have a number of different reasons for that: they don't have a driving licence, they hate traffic jams, there is no parking by their home or it's very expensive, they already own a nice set of wheels or have no desire for the additional monthly tax, that means a drastic drop in their net salary. What happens when an employer offers you a lease car and you don't want it? Perhaps a light bulb has gone off in your head: a car represents money that can be compensated in another way besides this gas-guzzler. How do you play the game?

1. Decide if it is actually realistic to refuse a car. For positions where there is a lot of travel, it would make it impossible, much too expensive or inefficient.

2. Which alternatives appeal to you? Cold cash? A train pass? A contract with a local taxi or car rental company?

3. Find out from the employer how much the monthly lease cost you are entitled to.
4. Make it clear to him that there are no hidden costs for you, such as your own monthly contribution for a car. Figure out what you monthly fuel costs would be for business travel and commuting. In brief, for a successful starting point in the negotiation game you must be able to produce a concrete amount.

A calculation

Imagine that the monthly cost for a lease car is £800. Adding fuel costs of, say, £100, that comes to a total of £900 per month. In addition, imagine you want to make a business trip by train and taxi once in a while and that for commuting nothing is better than the bus (in the bus lane!). What are the estimated monthly costs of commuting and business travel (which would be saved if you have the company car)? Let's assume that it totals to about £400. You are now talking about a cost to the employer of 900 – 400 = £500. You aren't unreasonable and can't predict the future perfectly. Therefore, you give the employer a leeway of £100. Hence, £400 per month is the negotiable cash alternative to the company car (taxable, of course).

Business expenses

These are a collection of small expenses that you need to make in order to do your job properly. The amount depends a lot on how high you are in the company and how often you have to work 'outside'. Examples of the kinds of expenses that you don't want to have to itemise to your boss (with all the extra administration this would involve) are for instance: coffee and alcoholic drinks that you buy for business relations here and there, parking fees, toll fees, telephone calls, meals that you serve at home to your business relations and so on. Much better to have a monthly expense allowance (along the lines of the contentious London living allowances afforded to MPs!). However, note that a general business expense allowance is a potential problem for the tax department, and runs the risk of being regarded as a taxable benefit if not substantiated. Check with your accountant or HMRC for details.

Travel costs

Commuting costs can be compensated in two ways:
1. The employer can pay a fixed amount per mile. It does not matter if you go by car, scooter, moped or foot.
2. The cost of public transport is reimbursed.

Note that any subsidisation of commuting costs will be regarded as a taxable benefit.

Telephone costs

It's appropriate to have your telephone costs reimbursed, if your job requires the use of your private phone. The tax department rarely accepts the subscription costs but do accept the calling costs or at least a part of them. Make sure that your declaration is realistic. When your monthly calls total on average £15, it would be difficult to declare £25 per month to your employer for your work related calls. You run the risk that you'll be found out. And that is never pleasant.

If the boss provides your mobile, then a fixed amount will be taxed every month since it's assumed that you will use it for private use as well. If you are really handy, then you will ask for two phones. The second mobile has to be used for business 90 percent of the time. Nothing is added on here but that won't make you any richer. It only starts getting interesting when your mobile is a smartphone or pocket-pc (pda, mini-computer), with Bluetooth, Wi-Fi, UMTS and other 'abbreviations' that you don't know the meaning of. The additional salary remains about the same but then you get a nice organiser with a lot more functions.

Internet costs

Your internet subscription or DSL costs are also negotiable. If your use is 90% business, which means work for your boss and not for yourself, then the amount can be added onto your payslip tax-free. The tax office isn't stingy about this. Nevertheless, most people would find it hard to prove that their private internet use is limited. When you keep your own private line, you will have a better argument for your boss and the taxmen.

Insurance

Sometimes you can negotiate with the employer for 100%, 50% or 25% of your health insurance costs. You may also negotiate a free annual medical check-up, paid for by your boss. Note that if your employer pays your health insurance, the tax office will treat this as a taxable benefit, and you will pay tax on this element of your income. The same principle applies to other types of insurance such as dental, life, risk, accident, liability, legal assistance, etc. (PS: How is an employer insured against workplace accidents? Is there insurance for your next of kin if you die? And what happens when you lose a finger in a meat-eating factory?)

Subsidised loan

The size of the loan that your employer is willing to grant you (when you ask!) will depend mostly on how big your salary is. The interest rate is often attractive; it is under the bank rate. If the HMRC think that the interest rate is unacceptably low (or is 0), you can expect a surcharge (they will treat the difference between interest paid and market interest rates as a taxable benefit).

Savings plans

More and more employers offer their workers the chance to participate in company savings plans.

Deferred Salary Leave Plan

In order to take a long vacation, take a period of leave, take early retirement or go on a 'sabbatical year', you can put money aside and save taxes via the deferred salary leave plan

Pension plan

Do you participate in the organisation's pension plan (or fund)? What are the costs and who pays for them? There are a number of different options at the negotiation table! Our experience shows us that very few people know what they have built up in their pension. When changing jobs to a new employer which offers an attractive salary but no pension, many are 'tempted' by the salary. However, if the pension is also taken into account, the lower salary with retirement savings may well be a better (or preferable) deal.

How much do you know about your pension plan? Test your knowledge by asking yourself the questions below that apply to you:

1. How much have you built up so far in pension entitlements with your previous employers?
2. How much pension can you build up with your current employer?
3. If you retire when you're 65, what will your total pension income be, including government pension?
4. You have an annual gross income of £45,000. What would your income be if you become 100 % disabled?
5. Imagine that you died. What would your next of kin receive in the form of your employee pension and other regulated funding?

You don't get any points or prize for answering these questions. Your reward is the chance to think critically about the unpleasant tasks and actions that need to be attended to!

Pensions have many facets and hidden problems. It is advisable in certain situations to seek professional advice instead of doing it yourself.

Bonus payments

These may be linked to the total company profits, the profits of your own section, your individual performance or a combination of all three. What is the company's policy? Do you find this reasonable? What are the expectations for the current or coming year? What are the past results like?

Tip

A bonus is always nice. But ask yourself if this is actually attainable. You can't plan a trip with your family to Madagascar with that tempting £10,000 bonus if no other colleague has ever achieved that.

Commissions

Negotiating commissions is a different story. Keep in mind that even a small amount like 0.5 percent can add up to a lot in terms of large turnovers after many years. Don't waste those half percentages!

When there is a commission, you can also think about an incremental scale and a provision for special actions, periods, products, services, etc.

Profit-sharing

Many companies offer some type of profit-sharing scheme for senior managers (and sometimes for all members of staff). Typically a proportion of the company's profits may be set aside for distribution either in cash or in shares to employees who participate in the scheme. Note that schemes involving the issue of shares are encouraged by HMRC which offers significant tax breaks on qualifying schemes, enabling recipients to defer or avoid tax on receipt of the shares, and to avoid any subsequent tax on disposal.

Tip

Profit is a splendid thing. However, can your (future) employer explain exactly what 'profit' means? Do you know how the profit payment is calculated? Have that specified in the employment contract, added as an appendix or defined in another way.

Many organisations have inflexible profit-sharing rules, that cannot be changed. However, you know that there are few matters in life that cannot change and if these rules can be bent for higher positions, you may be able to work out a better agreement as well ...or you'll stay poor.

Working hours

Is the right to flexible working hours negotiable? It is certainly worth the effort for some people to bring this up, when the organisation doesn't have a standard. For instance, we are thinking of employees with small children, two partners coordinating their working schedule, commuters wanting to avoid traffic jams, train travellers who need to work around the rail schedule, etc.

Teleworking

If this is an option for you? Discuss with your employer how much they can compensate you for your home office.

Training

This is becoming more and more important. Knowledge goes out of date quickly. In addition to your employer's own training schemes (and you should establish what these are) you may be able to negotiate financial support for training or educational activities which you undertake off you own bat.

Some organisations have a form of subtle coercion: if you earn your diploma (within a specified period), then you are compensated 100 percent; when you fail, it's nothing or 50 percent. More and more employers are drawing up an additional contract covering longer and more expensive educational courses. If the employee leaves the organisation within X number of years, then the tuition (sometimes tens of thousands of pounds!) has to be partially or fully paid back. That can inhibit your desire to leave. But you can also 'negotiate' your departure! Before you bring this up you must first find out what *exactly* those costs will be. Do textbooks count too? Excursion costs? Registration fees?

Termination

It may sound strange to talk about the terms of your eventual departure before you have even started working with your new employer, but there can be advantages to doing so. If the position is risky or insecure (perhaps subject to volatile or cyclical markets), you may be able to negotiate a premium payment in the event of redundancy or termination of your contract. For example, you might establish that if you are forced to leave the organisation within two or three years, you have the right to a certain buy-out premium or golden parachute (either a fixed amount or a proportion of your salary). At least you can ask whether this is negotiable!

In the event of redundancy, many employers will offer outplacement or recruitment consultancy support. Establish whether this is the case with your new employer.

These are obviously points to raise at an advanced stage in the discussions. It goes without saying that you don't *begin* your salary negotiations with questions about outplacement possibilities, vacations, free days, pension, early retirement and a sabbatical!

Tip

In negotiating to protect against adverse future developments, be careful you do not give the impression that you are a distrusting and indecisive person who wants to rule out all forms of risk!

Holidays

There are also several points that are negotiable regarding holiday entitlements:

♦ The number of days. There is a legal minimum number of days off but the maximum is subject to negotiation between the employer and employee.
♦ Can extra *unpaid* vacation days be included in the contract (for example to allow you to take a course of study)?
♦ How many vacation days have an obligatory date and how many are 'free-choice'? (Christmas, New Year's Day, etc.)
♦ Is an incremental scale discussable, so that you get one or more extra vacation days per year served.
♦ How many vacation days can you transfer to the following year?
♦ How many vacation days are you allowed to take in school holidays? Or do you hate taking holidays then? In that case, negotiate that you can get some fresh air outside of the school holidays.

Relocation

If you have to move for the new job, the moving costs can be part of the salary negotiation. Will 100 percent or 50 percent be reimbursed? Note that HMRC will allow up to £8,000 of relocation costs tax-free, subject to certain conditions (see http://www.hmrc.gov.uk/guidance/relocation.htm).

There are a number of costs associated with relocation, including costs of disposing of your current home, costs of acquiring your new home, removal costs, costs of connecting services, costs of equipping the new home (including furnishing and decoration) and so on. All of these costs should be covered or subsidised by your new employer.

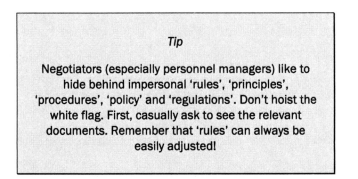

> **Tip**
>
> Negotiators (especially personnel managers) like to hide behind impersonal 'rules', 'principles', 'procedures', 'policy' and 'regulations'. Don't hoist the white flag. First, casually ask to see the relevant documents. Remember that 'rules' can always be easily adjusted!

Imagine you get a very attractive offer. You and your family have no problem with moving. However, you may have to sell your current home at a loss, which you had never anticipated. The extra costs eat away your savings and the increased income from the new job quickly disappears. You decide to keep the current job (and house). However, that will upset your potential employer. And the thought will keep gnawing away at you: is that a good decision? Be advised that some 'bosses' are prepared to make *your* losses *theirs*. That's a great point to negotiate!

Sabbaticals

In a few large organisations, senior executives may take a sabbatical year off once every few years. You are not allowed to look for another paid job during this period; the idea is that you will make yourself useful one way or another. That can be by doing research, studying, volunteering, writing, taking courses and the like. Saving for a leave of absence can be done by the already mentioned deferred salary leave plan. (Discuss the fine print with your personnel manager, accountant or tax adviser.)

Christmas bonuses

Some companies offer regular Christmas bonus payments (all taxable, of course!).

Payments in kind

The tax office will quickly deem any payment in kind as disguised salary. However, there are still some grey areas. In some sectors, it is difficult to get and hold good employees, with the normal salary, without offering these 'conditions'. Examples are children's education for teachers, healthcare for healthcare workers, cheap travel or accommodation in the hospitality industry and so on. Ask your new employer for details of any relevant schemes.

Company credit cards

A credit card makes life easier. Some employers routinely provide this piece of plastic to middle and senior managers. Note that expenses are likely to be carefully monitored, but there may be some types of expenditure (books, journals, entertainment, etc) which will be deemed allowable within certain pre-agreed limits.

Membership of professional organisations

The goal here is to keep or bring expertise up to date and to make informative contact with professional brothers and sisters. (Networking!) Not only you but also your future employer profits from it. It is not surprising that many organisations pay for these costs. But you have to ask for it!

Magazine subscriptions

A similar reasoning is used for the subscription costs of professional magazines. It is not unreasonable for the employer to pay these costs even when you receive these magazines at your home address. You can stay abreast of developments in your profession at your own convenience.

Club membership

There are companies, particularly in England and the United States, that pay for costly memberships to 'country clubs' and social clubs. The idea is that you can receive guests and meet new contacts at such clubs. Naturally the membership fee is treated by HMRC as a taxable benefit.

Company parking

It is always handy (especially with the increasing shortage of space) to obtain a company parking spot by your workplace. Why should you have to walk so far and drive around in circles (bad for the environment!) looking for a spot, if you can park in the garage under the office?

Day childcare/crèche

This not only increases your enjoyment in your work but it also gives you a peace of mind. Some employers provide day care or crèches themselves. Others may reimburse your costs, particularly if these are a condition of your being able to work for them.

Loyalty bonuses

Ask if there are any loyalty incentives. Naturally, you could also suggest a few. When you have worked there for X number of years, you may acquire the right to receive a pre-arranged number of 'virtual' shares, for example – you don't see these shares, only the positive difference in value between the share value at your time of joining and the value at your time of leaving (money in your pocket) – determined by the company accountant if necessary.

Fitness centre membership

People in the western world are getting fatter and heavier. More and more people are doing something about it by joining a fitness centre. Employers also believe in a good physical condition, since it decreases the chance of (sickness related) absenteeism. The ancient Romans knew that a healthy soul was housed in a healthy body. Interesting fact: in spite of that, the average lifespan of a Roman was 32 years. If your philosophy about 'wellness' matches your boss's philosophy, it's worth suggesting that the cost of a fitness club membership close to your home might be reimbursed by the company. First, find out about the costs (monthly or annual) before you bring this perk to the negotiation table.

Titles are cheap

Is a promotion a kind of a benefit? It may be nice to get a new title. It may give more status within one's organisation. And when you're applying for jobs, you have a snappier business card. But titles are also cheap. Your monthly salary specification won't necessarily change.

When are you satisfied and happy?

Keep in mind that money isn't everything. Just as important, or maybe even more important, are:

◆ pleasure in your work;
◆ the opportunity to develop;
◆ pleasant colleagues/team;
◆ little daily stress;
◆ limited (traffic jam-free) commuting;
◆ a boss you can talk to;
◆ interesting (socially meaningful) work;
◆ a good night's rest.

The choice is yours.

Tip

Be prepared. You may need a calculator during salary negotiations. Take it along in your pocket or briefcase.

Finding your way on the web

www.employeebenefits.co.uk
Latest developments and regulations governing employee benefits

www.ashworthblack.co.uk
Advisors on alternative remuneration structures, bonus schemes and employee benefits

www.hmrc.gov.uk/paye/exb-intro-basics.htm
Guide to the tax implications of different kinds of benefits

http://www.hmrc.gov.uk/guidance/relocation.htm
HMRC advice on relocation

5

The first interview

The job applicant's first contact with a completely new organisation is exploratory. You don't talk about detailed financial requirements at this stage, only general financial expectations regarding what is offered and what is sought. If these expectations are too dissimilar there is little reason for further talks – let alone negotiations. Both parties are wasting their time. In this chapter we will review how to lay the groundwork for salary negotiation at this early stage. The chapter will also be helpful for internal job applications, where a higher position is sought within the same organisation and the applicant needs to go through a general or special application process.

First the concept, then the cash

Very early in every job application procedure the question of salary must be addressed. Both the employer (Personnel Department employee, new boss or an intermediary) and you want to know what's in the offing financially. In the beginning, both parties stick out their antennae. Based on these first indications, the players know what the salary range will probably be and if further discussions are advisable. The salary on offer may be too low, or even, on occasion, too high (the employee may realise they are in the wrong ballpark).

In the following checklist, you will find questions that can be posed at the very beginning of the procedure. Don't confuse this with the salary negotiation. The goal of this list is to help you orientate yourself financially with a future employer. So you ask questions but you don't explain the reason behind them. You ask for information – you don't make any concrete demands. There are different techniques available for the later negotiations, which will be dealt with later. The information that you acquire in this part of the process will establish the first building blocks in the discussion about salary.

Keep it short and sweet at this stage. Make sure that there is first a love kindled between the two parties and that the engagement is announced.

After that, you can announce the marriage plans and draw up the marriage contract.

My future salary, a checklist

The following checklist contains main questions and sub-questions. The sub-questions are less important and go into more detail. Keep these for the subsequent salary negotiation.

Naturally, not all the noted questions are relevant for everyone. The list is also not entirely complete. Our tip: choose the questions that are relevant for you and your job application. Pick out the best ones. Avoid inciting annoyance by your barrage of financial questions. Be careful: this is the first orientation. First, you have to hook the fish, before you reel it in!

It's not necessary to ask all the questions listed here. The employer or his representative will spontaneously offer a lot of the information. When written information is available (salary scale, employment conditions, personal benefits statement, pension plan, etc.) try to get a copy so that you can read it at your leisure at home. You can ask detailed questions about it in a later conversation.

You might be afraid that asking all these questions may not please your interviewer. However, rest assured that they will value the fact that you are well prepared and that you won't let yourself be swindled. This attitude will have a positive effect on your work in the future. You'll be seen as someone who prepares himself thoroughly, has a positive critical attitude, has a good dose of perseverance and is a tough negotiator for the company.

You definitely don't have to feel unprepared when you're asked what you want to earn!

Checklist

1. Could you give me an initial provisional indication of the gross salary for this function?

♦ What is that amount based on? How is it determined?
♦ If there is a formal company payscale system, which scale do you want to place me in?
♦ What's the highest scale one can attain within five years?
♦ (Ask for a copy of the pay scales to take home.)

2. Does this organisation have profit sharing scheme?

♦ What is the idea behind it?
♦ What is the profit sharing based on?
♦ Is it based on the total company's results?
♦ Is it based on the individual's performance?
♦ Is it based on the group's or department's performance?
♦ Or is it based on all of these three points?
♦ Is it a fixed payment or a fixed percentage of one's income?

3. What kind of arrangement is there regarding commissions?

♦ What percentages are applied, and to what?
♦ Are there incremental scales?
♦ Is there an extra commission for special actions/periods/products/ services?

4. What can I expect my salary to be next year?

♦ Is that based on a standard increase or performance?

5. Is there any contribution towards travel costs?

6. Does a company car come with this position?

♦ Are there any agreements about the brand, model and class of car?
♦ How much is available for a (lease) car?
♦ Is one free to choose a car as long as it's within the budget?
♦ Can one buy the car from the leasing agency at the end of the contract period?
♦ If yes, at what price?

7. Does this organisation have a company (or group) pension scheme?

- ◆ (Ask for any brochures/regulations.)
- ◆ What are the conditions to participate?
- ◆ How much are the monthly contributions by both employer and employee?
- ◆ How flexible is this pension plan?
- ◆ What kind of assistance can the company provide in the case of existing non-transferable pension rights?

8. What kind of tax-free or tax-friendly rewards does this organisation offer?

9. Are business expenses paid and how high are they for this position?

10. Does this company offer a monthly payment towards home telephone costs? And what about mobile telephones?

12. Is there a company health insurance plan?

- ◆ (Ask for the overview regarding the conditions and premiums.)
- ◆ How much is the employer's contribution?

13. What other kinds of insurance are paid by the employer? (Dental, life, risk/accident, liability, legal assistance?)

14. Is it possible to arrange a mortgage through the employer on advantageous terms?

- ◆ And other kinds of loans?
- ◆ How advantageous are the conditions for employees?

15. What kind of company savings plans are there?

16. How is overtime compensated? (Beware: for many positions, this is considered part of the job.)

17. What training can they offer?

♦ Is there a departmental budget available for it? Per person?
♦ How many days are budgeted per person per year for training?
♦ What is the policy for participation in one day professional seminars and meetings?

18. How much does the company contribute towards any relocation costs?

♦ And for the decorating costs?

19. What sorts of payment in kind are available?

20. What kind of discount is given for the organisation's products/services?

21. Does the company pay the membership fees for professional organisations?

22. Are subscription costs for professional magazines (received at home) paid for?

♦ What kind of budget is available for this?

23. Does the organisation have an employee share scheme, or a share option scheme?

♦ What are the conditions for participating in it?
♦ Are these regular shares or special 'personnel shares'?

24. Are there any other employment benefits that I should know about?

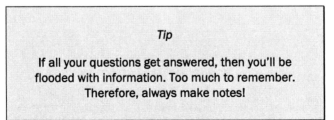

Tip

If all your questions get answered, then you'll be
flooded with information. Too much to remember.
Therefore, always make notes!

No financial information offered. Call!

What do you do if you come across an attractive job but can't find any information about the remuneration package, while a higher income is one of the reasons to change jobs? Our advice: make the phone call and dare to ask. Talk to the personnel manager, the director, department manager or the contact listed in the advertisement. Ask about the salary without any embarrassment since you want to know if it's worth your while to apply. Without this information, you may be wasting your own time and the employer's too. Making that phone call in the beginning offers a big advantage: when a pleasant conversation leads to an interview, then the other party will probably remember you. You are ahead of your competition!

Do you still remember your goal?

We have mentioned it earlier and we will mention it again later in the book: What do you want to achieve? What are your goals? What do you want to attain? You need to determine this first, if you don't want to end up like a lamb being led to the slaughter. However, all your goals need to be realistic and attainable. You may think that the new job needs to pay at least 20 percent more than your current one, but is this really achievable? And it may not yet be quite the time for that dream Ferrari in front of your house. A better approach is to ask yourself the following questions:

1. What can I accept as a minimum by a new job?
2. What is the maximum that I can expect? (In practice: 'the sky is the limit' applies only to astronauts.)
3. What can I realistically expect?

Result-based job descriptions

Some employers have already determined which salary scale the new employee will fall under based on a job rating system. If the company you are talking to does not have such a system then you have an advantage.

The first step is to set down a **job description** for your *current* position – preferably a result-based one. You need to show the other party what your strong points are. If you are applying for your first full-time job, try to represent your most recent work or study experience in the same way.

Remember that in almost every job application process the employer will look at the applicant's most recent achievements. These will provide a more reliable indicator of experience and ability than anything else.

What follows is an example of achievements in a result-based job description for an administrative position:

Supervision of employees and delegation of tasks for each employee according to his/her job description

♦ evaluation and control of work;
♦ monitoring of punctuality and thoroughness;
♦ seeing that work is completed on time.

Proposal of cost-saving steps, having asked all the department managers for cost reduction suggestions within their department

♦ In cooperation with them, testing the effectiveness and profitability of suggestions;
♦ recommending the best suggestions;
♦ finding methods to shorten the period between delivery and payment;
♦ thinking of the cheapest method to collect unpaid bills.

Perhaps some of these activities have led to great cost savings. The applicant's contribution to the company is thereby shown with concrete examples.

Be aware during your preparations that a good interviewer will ask hard follow-up questions: 'How did you achieve that exactly?' 'What kind of resistance did you have to deal with?' 'How did the management reward this?' And so on.

Do you want to get going with these preparations? Make use of the lists in chapter 4. (Found in the paragraph 'Supporting the arguments!') Write down which results you have achieved, preferably in terms of money.

Finding your way on the web

http://content.monster.co.uk/section323.asp
Job interview advice

73

6

Thinking of leaving?

Having looked at the job applicant in the last chapter, we are now going to turn our attention to the employee thinking of leaving. Almost all job holders at some time will ask themselves: Should I stay with my current job or is it better to leave? If so, where to? These questions may be prompted by a whole host of reasons, some negative and some positive. On the other side of the coin, a boss can also put out a feeler and ask if your present job is what you want. In this case the issue is likely to be: How well do you fit into the organisation?

How strong is your position? One way to find this out is the periodic performance appraisal interview, which takes place in most organisations. However, you can also assess your value and power within the organisation yourself.

In this chapter we will examine when it is smart to stay and when it is time to move on – and what sort of decision processes you need to adopt to make sure you make the right choice – and get the right salary outcome.

Decision based on negative reasons

It's obviously a good idea wherever possible to make a important career decisions for positive reasons. Think about the 'big challenge' that awaits you, new responsibilities, a bigger salary, more status, etc. However, the decision to leave a current job is inevitably often based on negative reasons, and these can be just as valid as positive reasons for change. Negative reasons for moving on include the following:

The work itself

You may be dissatisfied with your present job. Perhaps you find it boring, you do routine tasks, the challenge and excitement has disappeared, and the work is not enjoyable any more (whatever that vague feeling precisely should be). Perhaps the work has become too difficult (too many tasks, too little time). Perhaps the nature of your work has changed. The job may have become too computerised or desk-bound. There may be too much travel – or too little! Perhaps your company is relocating and there is pressure on you to move. Perhaps the commute is getting you down.

Yourself

Of course, you are constantly changing, yourself. Your ambitions may have grown too big for the current employer. Perhaps you have encountered a glass ceiling, with no ability of getting to the next level. The opposite can also be true: perhaps your initial ambition and drive have waned. It's just not so important anymore. Perhaps you feel differently now about the sort of work you are doing. Perhaps you have developed a new insight or business vision which your current employer does not (or would not) share.

Relationships at work

Conflicts may have arisen between you and your boss which you can't resolve. Perhaps there has been an organisational change which has disrupted your internal network. Perhaps competition with colleagues for a promotion or an assignment has caused unpleasant tensions – or worse, you feel you have been passed over for that promotion.

Takeover

Perhaps your company has been taken over by a competitor and you don't want to have anything to do with it. Or your position has been made redundant as happens in so many mergers – whether or not there are too many employees.

No more room for growth

You may be at the top of your salary ladder. Alternatively, the yearly profit sharing that you enjoyed is now a thing of the past and the chances of earning a profit in the coming five years is zero. You can't learn any more professionally. This employer no longer wants to invest in your training and education. There are no other possibilities that make your work interesting such as job rotation.

Personal factors outside work

You may have personal reasons for leaving your current job which are entirely unrelated to your work. Perhaps your partner has been offered another job and has suggested moving. Perhaps your divorce has come through, releasing you at last to start a new life somewhere else. Perhaps you want to move to live closer to your children (family, friends, acquaintances, a golf course and so on). Or the commuting time is too long because of the ever-increasing traffic jams.

The battle between heart and mind

Stay or go. That is the choice. A choice that often seems like a fight between the heart and the mind. Does a decision have to be made based on reason or must the heart have a say as well? There is no cut and dried answer. Obviously, decisions taken about important matters such as career development must be based on well thought-out arguments. (Who would dare to say 'My feeling is telling me to join company ABC'?) The next step in your career must be *carefully* considered. However, what is it that guides us most strongly in all the most important decisions in our lives? Our emotions are ultimately the deciding factor. As far as that is concerned we can compare the choice of 'stay or go' with accepting a marriage proposal. Is this carefully researched? Not always as much as perhaps it should be!

Employers and employees often make their final recruitment decisions based on emotions. (Don't believe it if they tell you any different!) Both parties look at the knowledge and skills in the first instance – the employer will assess the skills and competence in relation to other candidates, while the applicant will assess the opportunities and job characteristics (including pay) in relation to other possible jobs. But once the objective criteria have been met, the emotional considerations take over: Do employer and applicant *like* each other? Will the applicant 'fit' in the organisation? Is there trust and mutual respect? And so on.

As a job applicant, as the recruitment process draws to a close you will hopefully be saying to yourself: 'I have a feeling that I have a future in this company.' If not, do not take the job!

Intuition

It's well-known that employers place a lot of importance on their *subjective* assessments of job applicants – whether they seem to have the right character or temperament, whether they will fit in, and so on. Applicants, too, should use subjective assessment – because even when all the 'objective' factors are correct (great pay, no traffic jams, working in a lush green setting, chance for promotion, challenging work) if the company's culture doesn't appeal to you, then sooner or later you will feel trapped.

We enter here the world of intuition – an important idea that unfortunately is also rather vague. Job applicants need to be open to all kinds of signals from the interviewer(s) and the intended workplace – they need to listen to their own feelings, and also acknowledge them, which is not an easy task. They need to develop a third eye and ear, a kind of built-in radar.

If your intuition tells you a job will be 'right' for you (or 'wrong'), you ignore it at your peril!

Leave when it's good for you!

Many can talk about the interim 'grey' period when both the employer and employee contemplate a departure, but neither makes a move. The employee doesn't want to look for a new job right away; the employer doesn't want to directly fire him. However, both parties feel that the office drawer needs to be cleared out in the near future.

When you get into such a situation, our advice is simple: don't let yourself be driven out. Make decisions when they are good for you. Don't let yourself get put under (even more) pressure but keep your head cool. Set up your own plan and arrange everything carefully. You probably are in a relatively comfortable position in which the employer isn't worried about whether it's one day more or less. Make use of the time to carefully set out your career plan, if need be with the help of an expert. You will see that looking for a job is easier when you are employed than when you are unemployed. And that will also have consequences on the salary from the new employer.

Tip

There is a strong correlation between your training and your salary. In addition, knowledge and skills go out of date very quickly in the western world – you need continuous training to stay up to date. Make sure that you make use of training opportunities throughout your entire career. If an employer doesn't offer any, make the decision yourself to do something about it.

Are you still a favourite son/daughter?

How strong is your position in the organisation? The answer will obviously have a big influence on your decision whether to stay or to go. And on the size of your future salary. Ultimately, only the boss can answer this question. Unfortunately, for most of us, it is not possible to ask the question directly.

Big organisations have a system of periodic assessments and performance appraisal interviews. The reports of the interviews are signed by both parties and kept by the personnel department. Based on the reports you can figure out how you're seen within the company, at least through your assessor's eyes. When these kinds of interviews don't take place or when there aren't any reports, you will have to find out about your image through other channels.

Replacement premium

It costs most employers dearly to replace an employee. Think about the costs of recruitment (advertisement costs, agency costs, commitment of internal resource to selection and interview procedure, etc.) – not to mention the costs of induction and training after the position has been filled. Besides this, a new worker is inevitably less productive than the person they replace, and will continue to be so for some considerable time.

That means two things for you, as the person the employer may need to replace. In the first place, your employer's decision to let you go will not be made lightly (aside from possible legal issues). Secondly, there is a premium for you in the form of a small salary raise. It is much more advantageous to the employer to raise your salary than to look for a replacement. Bank that premium!

Maybe you can determine how much your replacement costs will add up to (for someone of your calibre in your sector)? That is great ammunition for the next salary negotiation!

> *Tip*
>
> **Ask yourself:**
>
> **1. How fast and/or easily can I be replaced? (A new assembly-line employee can be found and put to work very quickly; for a general manager the opposite is true.)**
>
> **2. What kind of influence do I have in the organisation? How 'important' am I, formally or informally? (For instance, think about your unique experiences or contacts.)**

Minimising risk

Imagine that you have made a decision to leave the firm where you have worked for years. You have built up a lot of benefits and privileges in that time. You should try to negotiate the value of these into your new contract (with your new employer) and also try to get some insurance in case the new job doesn't work out (you don't want to lose all the security you have built up in one fell swoop!). Here are some guidelines for negotiation with the new employer:

1. Keep in mind that all the conditions in the contract are always negotiable.
2. You should only sign a contract if all your rights have been carefully laid down. You can never be too critical when it comes to a contract you're offered.
3. Depending on the position, it may be possible to negotiate a golden parachute clause (for emergency landings) – a clause that promises hefty compensation if you are fired or made redundant after a short period of time. This clause doesn't cost the future employer a penny as long as you stay with the business. It's only when you get treated like a losing football trainer that the provision is applied. What should this 'life insurance' entail?
   - duration: for instance, applicable when your boss wants to replace you within two years;
   - compensation: for example a year's salary or a fixed amount;
   - automatic release from any non-competitive clause which may be in the contract.

4. If the new job does disappear unexpectedly, you may not have time to find a new position before you are forced to leave. Put a clause in your employment contract regarding the provision of outplacement services to help you find a new position. For example: in the event of redundancy, the employer will offer you the services of an agreed outplacement agency (or an outplacement agency of your choice), to help you secure another position. The duration of the outplacement programme would be for a minimum of 6 months (ideally for a year), during which time your salary would continue to be paid. Exaggerated? An unnecessary luxury? That is up to you to decide.

Taking a pay cut

Sometimes taking a step backwards is not a bad decision. But when it means a decrease in income, most people aren't too keen on it. Here is some advice for anyone who wants to take a lower-paid position:

1. Think about the new position. Is the associated salary loss worth it? And keep in mind that the new employer will see it as a sign of weakness if he knows you have relinquished some of your salary. He may judge that you are accepting you have a lower value to the company.
2. Establish what the minimum amount is that you can accept for the reduced position. Ideally this should be at least the equivalent of your current monthly gross salary without benefits. Imaging you are keeping your salary and giving up benefits. Why would you give up *all* the employment benefits, rights and security that you have acquired over the years?
3. Remember that the gross monthly salary that you bring into the negotiations (i.e. the salary you ask for) must be significantly higher than your minimum amount required. Base your argument on the market value, the overtime, the uncertainty, the fact that there is no (financial) growth in the position, etc.

Be good to yourself: keep a diary

Convince your boss to give you a raise by flooding him or her with facts that prove you are a valuable asset for the organisation. But don't leave it to the last minute to assemble your arguments. Imagine, your salary review is coming up and you have to prepare your case. If you don't have the records to hand, you must rely on your memory for examples of positive achievement, but 12 months can seem a long time – you will have to dip so deep into your memory to find ammunition that you may easily get discouraged. And there is such an easy solution: the diary method.

Make notes of all important events at work that you've dealt with and keep them in a binder. Get the binder out of the cupboard just before you have your performance appraisal interview or salary review and make a summary of your accomplishments for your boss. You will surprise yourself how often you have proved- your worth.

Each diary page can have the following information:

◆ Date:
◆ Achievement/activity:
◆ Result (as concrete as possible, for instance in amount of time saved, profit or cost savings, decrease in complaints, faster information by employees, etc.):
◆ Effect of results (new ideas, what the results have led to, etc.):

NB: You don't have to literally keep track of what you have achieved every day.

Threatening to quit?

It is sometimes tempting to threaten to quit when the first signals indicate that you're not going to be offered a reasonable salary raise. Is that a good strategy? No! Let us explain why:

1. Unless you really intend to carry out the threat, it is a big risk. What if your boss replies 'Okay, leave then – I'll get my secretary to draft a letter of resignation for you to sign'?
2. If, out of necessity, you back down, by taking back your words, then you have lost your credibility forever (regarding salary).
3. It is a confrontational strategy which can also smack of disloyalty – not a good platform for an ongoing relationship with your boss.
4. Imagine that you *do* manage to get a raise using this approach. What strategy are you going to use next year?

> **Tip**
>
> Never let yourself be tempted to combine a performance appraisal with a salary discussion. You run the risk that your performance will be deliberately presented in a negative way. Then the employer can say: 'You understand that due to the problems we've just discussed there is no way we can give you a raise.' During a performance interview you need to have the freedom to discuss, among other things, what kind of help you need to get from the organisation (your boss, colleagues and others) in order to perform better. This is difficult to do when you also want to bring up financial matters.

Finding your way on the web

www.cipd.co.uk/subjects/perfmangmt/appfdbck/perfapp.htm
Chartered Institute of Personnel and Development advice on appraisals

www.admin-ezine.com/performance_appraisals_toc.htm
An ezine review of appraisal strategies for employees

www.i-resign.com/UK/resigning/
Advice on how to quit or resign

7

The preparation:
knowing yourself and your opponent

In almost all successful salary negotiations the following are true:

1. *The negotiation is carried out between 'partners' (employer and employee) who have had or will develop a long-term relationship.*
2. *One hardly ever tries to swindle the other (logical, considering the first point).*
3. *Negotiations are almost always carried out in a friendly and courteous manner. And that is also not surprising considering the circumstances.*
4. *The rules of the game are clearly established and understood. There is a logical structure to the negotiation. Each party presents his proposals and counter-proposals in an orderly sequence. When a party has just lowered his price, he won't try to raise it after only a few seconds. An offer is an offer.*

What can we learn from this? When both parties enter into a discussion, they each will want to find a win-win situation. Why would you turn your future boss into your enemy? That's not the right strategy to adopt, to put it mildly. You should see the negotiation as an opportunity to establish a basis for future co-operation. And once a relationship is established, then both parties will want to maintain it.

Part of the preparation is to get ready mentally to enter the negotiation arena, to 'think it through' in advance. Always keep in mind that the employer, at least during the negotiation, is your opponent. He probably has more experience concerning negotiating than you. He can put you in an uncomfortable position by posing many difficult questions. You have to draw your strength from your thorough preparation.

What authority does your opponent have?

Nothing is more annoying than negotiating with someone who does not have the authority to make an agreement. In other words: your negotiations have resulted in an attractive agreement but, unfortunately, the contract is not ratified by the captain of the ship. He says that the sailor has promised things which he has no authority to promise. All that effort was for nothing.

You have to be clear in advance of the negotiation whether or not the results with the negotiator have any value. If you have any doubts, let him clearly spell out that he has the authority to make decisions, so that he can't hide behind other people!

A prickly and somewhat avoidable situation is the following: You negotiate with your (future) boss. After a period of time you have reached an agreement about your remuneration package for the coming year. The boss shakes your hand and says: 'Human Resources will finalise the details.' You breathe a sigh of relief. The battle was quickly over. But Human Resources doesn't finalise the details. The Human Resources manager asks you to see her. After greeting you, she lets you know that the agreement you've just made isn't possible. It doesn't follow the internal procedures, rules, agreements and so on. 'Sorry, but your boss should have known that.'

This story hasn't ended yet. You decide to confront your boss and discuss the problem. (Whose problem is it, actually?) The head of your department smartly remarks: 'Human Resources only has an advisory role. I decide who to hire for my department, what their responsibilities and tasks are and how they are rewarded. You tell that to Mrs Big from Human Resources!' So you end up being sent around in circles. And on your way back to Human Resources, you think about how in this company the humans and the resources don't have much in common.

It is also not easy when both your boss and the HR employee are sitting across from you at the negotiation table. You are in the minority for everything. The only advantages are quick decisions and actions.

Tip

When negotiating for a new job, ask what position your discussion partner holds and who will negotiate the salary. The manager may need to refer to a third party for this. Or it may be the manager's tactic to toss the ball back and forth in order to avoid having difficult discussions with you about salary.

When to negotiate?

When is the best time to have salary negotiations? Are certain days or times preferred? (Never during your boss's rush hour!)

Important for tactical negotiators: some people function better in the morning, others in the afternoon or evening ('morning person', 'night owl'). When you know that your opponent is at his best in the evening, try to arrange a meeting early in the morning. If you succeed, you'll be a step ahead right away!

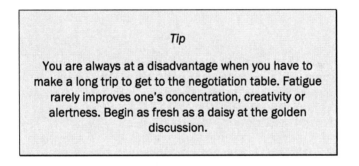

> ***Tip***
>
> **You are always at a disadvantage when you have to make a long trip to get to the negotiation table. Fatigue rarely improves one's concentration, creativity or alertness. Begin as fresh as a daisy at the golden discussion.**

Negotiating a raise

Some people who are hoping for a raise in their current position may think it's difficult to 'bother' their boss about something as insignificant as their salary. They are embarrassed about it, don't want to come across as a money-grubber or find the topic somewhat burdensome. Or maybe they have had bad experiences in the past. There are two unpleasant situations where there will be little chance of success. We will describe them and how you can defend yourself against them.

Scenario 1

Your boss has little or no time. He runs around like a headless chicken and discussing your salary is not at all important (maybe because it's so high, maybe because it's so low). For whatever reason, you get the message that it's not discussable. Intimidated, you don't feel you have the courage to pin your boss down – but you want a resolution. What do you have to do to get your self-respect back and to improve your monthly salary?

The answer is to request an appointment – by phone, by email, or preferably in person. Say that it will take 30 to 60 minutes of his valuable time and say what you want to discuss. When a time and date has been set, confirm again that he can free up this time. If he lets on that it could be a problem, make another appointment since you want to be able to discuss this important matter in an unhurried manner. It's not possible during the week? Why not in the weekend? Is it a problem during the day? Then a 'breakfast date' or a meeting in the evening? In short, there is always an hour free sometime. Only the very worst managers don't have any time for their people. And you know what happens to these managers sooner or later.

Scenario 2

You have made an appointment and the day before the meeting the boss's secretary calls up very apologetically to say that he can't make the appointment and has to cancel. He will get back to you. What now? You make a new appointment right away. You are not concerned that the salary discussion will be cancelled; but your boss will be concerned if this keeps happening. You clamp your jaw onto your boss like a fox terrier, until you finally get that desired appointment. If he keeps avoiding you, you'll have to go higher up. If there aren't any higher levels in the organisation, then you should draw your own conclusion.

Tip

Your boss goes on holiday and then you do. (Two months pass.) There are business and internal company trips, congresses, seminars, illness, you name it. Time flies when you're not having fun, too.

Psychological profile of your opponent

Naturally you don't have the opportunity to put together a psychological profile (whatever that entails) of your opponent. You are in good company:

the police and army, who have to hire experts to profile terrorists' and kidnappers' personalities, have a lot of difficulty with it as well.

If you know how the other person ticks, then you will probably know what his Achilles heel is. It is improbable that as a job applicant you will get down to negotiations during the job interview. Try to find out as early as possible who you will have to negotiate with or reach an agreement with. Make notes about his personality. With the ever more sophisticated search engines on internet, you will be surprised what you can learn about people!

Take time at home to fill in the list below after your first interview, so that you have an advantage going into the next round of discussions. A bit over the top? The more resources you have to increase your salary the better, in our opinion.

	Apply to my opponent (check off)			
	completely	*a little*	*Not*	*don't know*
Calm	☐	☐	☐	☐
Business-like	☐	☐	☐	☐
Flexible	☐	☐	☐	☐
Describes things accurately	☐	☐	☐	☐
Listens well	☐	☐	☐	☐
Convincing	☐	☐	☐	☐
Dominant (controls the conversation)	☐	☐	☐	☐
Can put things into perspective	☐	☐	☐	☐
Knows his business	☐	☐	☐	☐
Critical	☐	☐	☐	☐
Deals with things systematically	☐	☐	☐	☐
Cooperative	☐	☐	☐	☐
Trustworthy (reliable)	☐	☐	☐	☐
Independent	☐	☐	☐	☐
Has authority	☐	☐	☐	☐
Spontaneous	☐	☐	☐	☐
Alert	☐	☐	☐	☐
Creative/inventive	☐	☐	☐	☐
Pays attention to my non-verbal signals	☐	☐	☐	☐
Ambitious	☐	☐	☐	☐
Persistent	☐	☐	☐	☐
Views himself positively	☐	☐	☐	☐
Disciplined	☐	☐	☐	☐
Feeling of responsibility	☐	☐	☐	☐

Efficient	☐	☐	☐	☐
Practical	☐	☐	☐	☐
Decisive/resolute	☐	☐	☐	☐
Humble/shy	☐	☐	☐	☐
Detailed/precise	☐	☐	☐	☐
Other	☐	☐	☐	☐
....	☐	☐	☐	☐

Your opponent's worries

Do you think that negotiating is difficult for you? That's right! But your opponent also has his problems. Try standing in his shoes for a change:

1. If your opponent sees himself as a fighter and wants to keep up the tough guy image, fighting with you for every penny, it's a good idea to let this kind of negotiator blow off some steam in the beginning. When this type has settled down you can take over the discussion. Let the other party win the emotional judo match – as long as your wishes are granted.
2. Your opponent will inevitably have to worry about precedents. If you get most of what you want, then it's the end of the story for you, but it's not the end of the story for the other side of the table. Your opponent knows that (future) colleagues will make the same demands sooner or later. If you are pushing for an unusual agreement which might be perceived as setting a difficult precedent be flexible in trying to find a 'face-saving' solution.
3. It's possible that the other party has put in a good word for you to his boss and has made it clear that you'll be getting the job. You only have to dot the 'i's and cross the 't's. If the 'deal' doesn't go ahead then your discussion partner will lose face. The more he has praised you, the bigger a problem it will be. You are in fact his investment and he will want to guard it in Fort Knox. Besides, how often can a manager allow himself to lose a good (future) employee over something like (a small difference in) salary?

Kinds of questions

Research has shown that good negotiators listen. They don't need to dominate the conversation. Let the opponents 'talk themselves in a corner'. Then the listener has time to think things calmly through!

If you only ask 'closed' questions that can be answered with a simple 'yes' and 'no', then you'll make it very easy for your conversation partner. Ask as many open questions as possible. These questions begin with 'how', 'what', 'when', 'why' and so on. For example: 'How come all your possibilities are already exhausted?' Or: 'What can you offer me as far as extra training is concerned?' Or: 'What kind of raise can you give me?' In this way you force the other party to give you specific answers!

Keep on asking questions

Don't be embarrassed when you don't understand something. Repeat your question! What's the worst that can happen? Or ask questions like:

♦ 'What do you mean?'
♦ 'Can you explain that again?'
♦ 'Could you please be clearer/more specific?'
♦ 'What should I understand by that?'
♦ 'Can you give me an example?'
♦ 'I am afraid that I don't understand you completely (could you explain).'

Asking questions is important and listening to the answers even more so. In chapter 8 you will find principle 1: listen carefully and attentively.

Frequently made mistakes

Mistakes are made quite often during salary negotiations. We'll take the bull by the horns so that you can avoid making those errors.

Fight for status

Both parties stand across each other like proud peacocks. One of them (or maybe both) is willing to give in on one of the points but is afraid of losing face or of being seen as super smart, macho or something else. The result? A long, exhausting, irritating fight with probably two losers.

Cost-benefit analysis

Negotiations go into overtime. Your difference is minimal, but you are not making any progress. Then admit it. The potential benefits do not justify the costs of going further with the negotiation. And by costs we also mean the other party's irritation.

Group negotiations

It is especially difficult to negotiate with a group (for example, HR staff, your future boss and his director). Try to avoid this unfair battle – perhaps by suggesting to your future boss that you would prefer to discuss terms privately with him, before bringing in the others.

Bluffing

Poker is a pleasurable nightly pastime and may be an effective way to earn some money under the table. But its place in salary negotiation is doubtful. If your acting talent isn't up to it, you could be playing with fire.

How 'reasonable' is 'reasonable'?

Negotiators often use terms such as 'reasonable' and 'fair' as artillery in the battle – fine-sounding words which have little concrete meaning. Always ask for further explanation: 'Reasonable, what are you measuring that against?' Or: 'Who determines what reasonable is?' Other sample sentences: 'I am happy that you want to be reasonable/fair (are a reasonable person). I value that. But as I see it, based on the salaries that are being offered (in the automotive sector, my former work, etc.), my salary demands are also reasonable.'

How friendly do you have to be?

When you agree to the employer's first and best (best???) offer, you're being very nice. But you are probably losing money – not only now, but in your further career with this organisation as well.

Tip

It is very pleasant when the future employer invites you out for lunch or dinner during the negotiation rounds. A good glass of wine will especially help to build up a relationship. Even though the other party pays for the meal, it may cost you more in the long run.

Creativity

In many negotiations, the parties have fixed views of what they are trying to achieve and may not be prepared to deviate from their own points of view. This inflexibility can cause negotiations to fail. The solution it to apply creativity in finding a way to marry the differing perspectives.

It's too bad that we can't teach you creativity in a few lines, but we can inspire you to solve a negotiation problem by being creatively critical:

- Suggest alternative types of remuneration or benefits which might appeal to the employer and which are not already on the table.
- Play with time; there's no rule that says that you have to get a raise on 1 January (instead of January 10 or 15, or February 24). What do think about two smaller raises in January and July?
- Working with the same theme: a part of your pay can be paid out at a later date, such as with the savings plan or a contribution to your deferred salary plan.
- What can you offer? To work longer days, more overtime, a personal contribution to certain insurance plans or the company car, not taking a number of vacation days, taking on additional tasks, etc.
- Is there a possibility to push some tasks forward or do some more quickly?
- How can you save costs? Do you have any influence on this?
- Are there any other ways you can increase profitability of the business?
- Are there any other activities in the business which you could perform less expensively than the current operatives?
- Imagine you have to start the negotiations all over again. What would you do differently?
- Are there any temporary solutions that can be discussed?
- Get a hold of old contracts (your own, or contracts negotiated by friends, colleagues etc). Maybe these will give you some ideas.

Answering those difficult questions

During your salary negotiations you can expect difficult and awkward questions. A lot depends on your preparation and of course your experience. If you are prepared for an unpleasant question, you will already have practised with one or more suitable answers – and you won't act like a dreamy zebra that has just bumped into a not unkind but unfortunately overenthusiastic and hungry lion.

Below we set out a series of sample questions, with the reason for asking it, and a selection of model answers that will help your negotiation. (Some answers are more direct than others; choose the answer that fits your personality, style and position.) You now have a powerful instrument to get through the negotiations unscathed, and assertively!

Question 1. 'What is your current (gross) (monthly/annual) salary?'

Objective of the question: This can be an innocent question but be careful! The employer will probably want to know a few things, not necessarily in this order:

1. Can we afford this candidate?
2. Will the ultimate salary fit into our compensation structure (agreements, traditions, rules, budgets)?
3. Is the candidate knowledgeable about this labour market? Does he know his own worth? In other words: has the candidate sold himself well?
4. Does the cited salary fit with the education, experience, current position and so on? To put it another way: is this candidate speaking the 'truth'?

Your answer: Before you consider bluffing, remember that your P45 will clearly state the amount you have earned in the current tax year. You can bluff a little about the value of benefits, but you will need to be straight on the question of gross salary. You could deflect the question initially by saying: 'What is important for me is the total package: gross salary and benefits; in short, what I can earn now and in the future (pension!). This is obviously a complex calculation but I would say my total package at the moment is worth about £xxxx.' (Here a little poetic license may be allowable.)

If you normally receive annual bonus or commission payments, you can try: 'Including annual bonus/commission I would expect to earn in the region of £xxxx before tax this year.' (Again, this leaves a little room for manoeuvre, if you can plausibly inflate your bonus expectations.)

Question 2. 'Could you please send me a copy of your most recent payslip?'

Objective of the question: An efficient way to see if you are telling the truth or not! The employer can figure out how much you're worth to your current employer down to the last penny.

Your answer: You could refuse to cooperate since you feel it's an invasion of your privacy, but this would almost certainly lose you the job! As mentioned in 1. above, they are going to find this information out anyway from your P45. The most you can do is stall: 'Yes, of course. If we reach agreement I will happily provide with any supplementary information required.'

Question 3. 'What benefits (perks) are you currently receiving?'

Objective of the question: refer to question 1.

Your answer: Refer to question 1 (and 2 if needed). If desired, talk about the verbal agreements that are not covered in the employment contract and/or salary slip. A few examples (which are important for a new job): a half day per week off for study leave, a yearly visit to an American conference, profit sharing, a career path with periodic promotions, partial payment via a foreign subsidiary, etc.

Question 4. 'Are you prepared to receive a substantial portion of your income as commission or via a profit-sharing arrangement?'

Objective of the question: The employer can ask this for three reasons. Firstly: are you someone who is willing to stick out your neck, without getting it into the noose? Or do you want all the security (and maybe 'peace of mind' at the end of the month)? Secondly: do you have self-confidence? Do you think you can influence your performance and income? Thirdly: the employer may want to shift part of his financial risk to you. If the company is doing poorly then you will share in the downturn.

Your answer: Of course, this depends a lot on why you think the question is being posed, as well as your own willingness and ability to take risks. And of course you can make a counter-offer: 'How well is taking risks rewarded here?'

In general, commercial employers want to have entrepreneurial employees who are self confident and willing to take risks!

Question 5: 'What is more important for you: a high fixed salary with lower profit-sharing based on your own performance or a low fixed salary with higher profit-sharing?' ('And why would you make that choice?)

Objective of the question: The reasons for this question are similar to the previous one. They want to get assess your temperament: do you choose security or are you a 'gambler'? Besides this, the answer of this question can also have financial consequences for the employer: can he afford you?

Question 6. 'Do you know that things are not going that well financially for us at the moment?'

Objective of the question: this can be an honest question seeking to warn you of the circumstances before you accept the position. However, it is more likely to be designed (1) to test your mettle (are you willing to accept a challenge to help reverse the company's fortunes) or (2) as a basis for a low salary offer.

Your answer: You can thank them for the cup of coffee and say good-bye. It's better to ask for specific information; is the turnover sagging, is it a temporary dip or is there a clear downward trend, are there problems by the subsidiaries? It could be that everything is better than expected.

If the answers are disappointing you may want to consider leaving this employer or not accepting a job there. Or, depending on the company's evident performance, get a modest salary raise three or four times a year. Another option: accept a lower salary for the first twelve months in favour of a much higher salary the next year. Your loss can be nicely compensated this way. (Make sure it's written down!)

Question 7. 'Where did you get your information about the industry rate for this position? I would like to see your figures.'

Objective of the question: It could be that the employer doesn't have that information but he could also know exactly what the salaries are around the country. He is either asking the question to get information from you or he doesn't trust you. Have you bluffed and just said something?

Your answer: You could agree to send the requested tables since you have them. Or name the website where you can find them. If you are bluffing you will have to keep it up! Ask the employer which figures he has, so that you can compare them with yours. It could be that both salary scales are closer than you first thought. (There is no precise information on business jobs anywhere!)

Question 8. 'That is a low salary for someone your age (and/or with your experience). Why is that?'

Objective of the question: The HR manager, or whoever poses this question, has two reasons for asking this. Firstly he suspects you are being underpaid, in other words you have undersold yourself in the past. (This is not in your favour!) Secondly, it is possible that there is a reason that you are not earning much: your performance is inadequate or you're under-qualified.

Your answer: You know that both reasons are negative. How can you turn this around? You have a number of options here. You can differentiate between salary (indeed rather low) and other kinds of payment, many free days and great profit-sharing. Or you make a lot of use of the internal and external training possibilities that the organisation offers. (You are well advised to prove that.)

Or turn the discussion in a positive direction by pointing out that your current employer hates to pay top salaries but it has been a great place to learn, not only because of the formal training (refer above) but also because of the varied practical experience. You have invested a lot in yourself! A third possible answer: disagree. You aren't being underpaid. Whether you're believed depends on how knowledgeable the employer is.

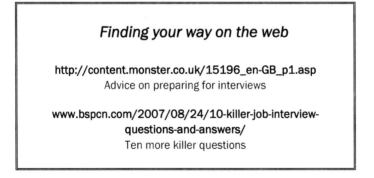

Finding your way on the web

http://content.monster.co.uk/15196_en-GB_p1.asp
Advice on preparing for interviews

www.bspcn.com/2007/08/24/10-killer-job-interview-questions-and-answers/
Ten more killer questions

8

Your cast-iron salary-negotiating system

Some people think that reaching a compromise during a negotiation means meeting each other half way. This is a simplistic view, to say the least. It reminds me of the man who has his head in a deepfreeze and his feet in boiling water, and feels 'on average comfortable'. Average makes sense but what about comfortable?

For a negotiation to work, both parties have to have a bit of flexibility and leeway, and the will to reach an agreement. In this chapter we put the actual salary discussion into a framework, a model, which is easy to remember, practise and put to use. We assume that you are well prepared and ready to enter into negotiation. What you need is a systematic approach which embraces the core techniques and skills of successful negotiation. This model can be used in every salary negotiation and consists of five principles and five steps, which will be explained one at a time below.

Understand the psychology of the other party

Negotiators are people. You are not dealing with abstract company representatives, but with people who, just like you, have emotions, uncertainties, beliefs, values and personal histories. For instance it may be important to them to be liked; they may have a strong moral sense of fair play; they may react badly to confrontation; and so on. Even with the most business-like negotiation partner, emotions will play a role. It is essential to pay attention to the human aspects of negotiation as well as the purely practical.

Separate the personal from the business. Try to establish a personal rapport, and do not take any setback, contradictions or rejections personally.

Your opponent will naturally have a different perspective from yours. Put yourself in his shoes and imaging how he will be thinking about each of the issues you raise. Try to establish a mutual approach:

- 'I understand that you are tied to the salary scales but let's investigate which possibilities there are in the higher scales.'
- 'It's clear to me that this is not an easy situation and that you have already tried before. But let's look how we can solve this problem together.'

Sometimes emotions are used (anger, grief) to put pressure on the opposing negotiator.

If you are surprised, offended or provoked by something he says, ask yourself:

- Why did he say that? (Could he have said it or worded it in a different way, or not?)
- What could be his ulterior motive for making this remark?
- Is something bugging him? What is it?

The salary negotiation model

There are five core principles of negotiation set out below. Regardless of where you are in the negotiation, you need to keep these five principles in mind and put them into practice *throughout* the negotiation:

- Principle 1: listen carefully and attentively;
- Principle 2: be concrete and assertive;
- Principle 3: remain persistent;
- Principle 4: always keep the interest of the employer in mind;
- Principle 5: don't give anything away for free.

Alongside the five core principles, there are five key steps to successful negotiation. Follow these steps in chronological order, from beginning to end, while observing the five principles, and you will achieve your objective:

- Step 1: take the initiative;
- Step 2: let the employer speak;
- Step 3: explain your own negotiable points;
- Step 4: discuss the possible differences;
- Step 5: reach an agreement.

Five principles you need to know

Principle 1. Listen carefully and attentively

It's a good idea in every conversation to listen to what the other person has to say. This is especially true in a negotiation. Listening carefully is often more important than speaking.

Everyone, including the negotiator on the other side, needs *attention* and wants to be recognised and valued. Besides that, some will want to have their authority recognised and acknowledged. Listening plays an important role in doing this. Research shows again and again that listeners are valued.

Listening is not easy. It is a verb – it doesn't happen on its own! If you want to know what someone else is thinking, why he made a particular (perhaps nasty) remark, you will have to ask questions and then listen well, otherwise important information will slip right past you!

How do you interrupt?

You may have to deal with a friendly but dreadfully wordy negotiator. What do you do then? First of all, remember that some people enjoy to talk a lot and they often have a lot of informative things to say. The best tactic is to calmly let the other person speak. It may take a long time, but you will get all the information you need. And time isn't money for you yet! Besides, if you interrupt the interviewer, you run the risk of annoying them. In addition, you will miss the chance to gain *sympathy*, needed for a long-term and pleasant working relationship.

What weapons do you have if your interviewer is continuously talking but saying nothing of value (low level of information)? This could be a tactic to create a lack of time in order to avoid negotiations or to hide problem areas. (We will discuss this point later.) Or are you dealing with someone who just likes to talk? Or is it a technique to put you at ease?

When there is little time available for your salary negotiation (on purpose?), so that decisions need to be made quickly, you will be forced to get the other person on the 'right track' and to keep them there.

Interrupting doesn't have to be rude. Make use of the following friendly sentences when you want to regain the initiative:

♦ 'Sorry for interrupting but I would like to know if...'
♦ 'I'm sorry to have to interrupt but I believe we haven't talked about ... yet'
♦ 'I agree with you, but I also find that...'
♦ 'That's really helpful/interesting. Could we go back to point 3 on our list?'

- 'You have said earlier that.... I would like to react to that.'
- 'Now, keeping to the point...'
- 'I would like to remark that...'
- 'May I summarise your reaction as...'

Make use of closed questions, questions that can only be answered with 'yes' or 'no', or restrict the possible answers in another way. For instance: 'What do you think: shall we make an appointment for a follow-up discussion now or shall we do that tomorrow?' (You know that the other party can't escape.)

A warning: The preamble to many salary negotiations often involves very little exchange of information. Both parties are sniffing each other out, testing the temperature, or trying to create the right mood for the discussion (friendly or formal, as the case may be).

Principle 2. Be concrete and assertive

Your gross salary and benefits are very concrete matters. How much do you want to earn? What is the maximum that the employer has in mind? How many vacation days are standard and how many are negotiable (on top of that)?

Try to keep the discussion focused on specific concrete, and quantified proposals. An example: 'First you proposed to reduce the gross salary by 10 percent. I agreed with that provided that I get a lease car and a personal education budget. Let's talk about the car. What brand and model were you thinking of?'

When you keep bringing up specific concrete proposals, it shows that you are well prepared. Although the interviewer may react defensively, he will come out of the talk with a positive impression of your effort and systematic approach.

Principle 3. Remain persistent

It is fairly easy during a salary negotiation to get lost in the swamps of accounting technicalities, tax considerations, profit-sharing mechanics and so on, and before you know it your time is up. Remain as persistent as a fox terrier. And your behaviour will be rewarded, literally.

If you are forced to relinquish (but not concede) a negotiating point (for example, business expenses), say that you want to go back to it – preferably in that very discussion. Make a note, so that you don't forget it in the heat of the battle!

Principle 4. Always keep the interest of the employer in mind

Are you there for the organisation or is the organisation there for you? We won't start a discussion about this but it is beneficial for you to put yourself in your employers' shoes during the whole negotiation process. 'If I was the boss and someone told me this or asked this question (in this way), how would I feel?'

You should maybe ask yourself once in a while: 'How does that help the employer? How will that work for him?' Keep in mind that the employer is also wrestling with those kinds of questions. Remember that the organisation could be worried about ripple effects: when they promise you something, then there is the chance that, within twenty four hours, colleagues will be standing on the sidewalk to get the same demand.

If you are seen to recognise the interest of the company, then you will give your discussion partner *peace of mind* and *security*. He will sleep softly and sweetly when you tell him you will effectively solve his sales management problem while you use it as a chance to grow.

Principle 5. Don't give anything away for free

December is the month for gifts. Christmas and Father Christmas are terrific opportunities to be generous. But stay on the receiving side of the salary negotiations. Before you start playing Father Christmas you need to think about three things:

1. Whatever you give away during the discussion, you will never get back. That is how the negotiation game works. Maybe you can try again next year but for now the point is lost.
2. Sometimes you may not know exactly what you're giving away. Imagine that a portion of your income depends on commission. In your negotiation you give away 1%. That may not sound much – just 1 penny in every pound. But the reality is that a 1% reduction in commission can represent a very high proportion indeed of your income. For example, if you accept 5% instead of 6%, than you are not handing over 1% but almost 17%! On sales of £600,000 you have just reduced your commission from £36,000 (6% of £600,000) to £30,000 (5% of £600,000) – a difference of £6,000 you have just given away. You could probably do some very interesting things with that money.
3. We have already said that a successful negotiation has implications for years to come. For instance when you have obtained a 5 percent salary increase, the following round (in a year's time) will be based on that increase.

Five simple steps you need to take

We're going to make it more difficult. As indicated above, you have to keep to a certain logical sequence to succeed in your salary negotiation (the five steps). We will now examine each of the steps, including also a range of smaller 'sub-steps'.

NB: Job applicants, follow this model **after** a job has been offered! This discussion model will give you enough support to tip the balance in your next salary negotiation in your favour. Practise it beforehand.

Step 1. Take the initiative

It is possible that your new employer will offer you a fantastic salary and great benefits right from the beginning. Do you still need to negotiate? The choice is yours. More often than not your wishes and the company's will not be entirely in sync (yet). The wrinkles have to be ironed out, or a somewhat harder approach may be needed. You need to take the initiative. If you are not offered the opportunity to talk about salary, request a meeting to have that conversation. In any event, you need to make your feelings clear. If you don't let them know what you think about the compensation, they will rightly think that you are satisfied with their first offer.

The same principles apply for existing employees seeking a raise, or seeking to improve their raise. If there is no standard procedure for salary review, request a meeting.

From experience we know that many employees, from the top to the bottom, have difficulty asking for a salary meeting. The result is that they walk around for weeks and sometimes months with an uncomfortable feeling of failure. We advise you to take the initiative, and call that meeting. At the beginning of the meeting, let them know in a few sentences what the purpose of the meeting (in your eyes) will be. Sentences that you can use are:

- ◆ 'As you know we are going to discuss my salary (for next year) this morning. I would like to explain my ideas and wishes about that.'
- ◆ 'I'm happy that you could come to this meeting. Just to set things straight: do we still have an hour to talk about my career and finances? Shall I begin?'

> **Tip**
>
> **If you have taken the initiative to set up a salary discussion, don't let the initiative slip out of your hands by needless talk about procedures, principles, rules and details.**

Look the other person straight in the eye. Don't 'play' with a pencil or anything else since this shows insecurity. (Refer to non-verbal communication.)

Do you talk about the weather to break the ice? That depends on your relationship with the other party. When you have known each other for years and work together a lot, then you can bring up a topic of mutual interest. But keep it short! In other situations it is better to get right down to business. You don't have anything to hide, do you? And you are fighting for an honourable and just purpose: a better income.

The tone you take will immediate influence your discussion partner's mood in a way that can make or break the negotiation. When your approach is friendly, he will also show his best smile. When you have an angry look on your face, you will be paid back with the same, to put it financially. The first notes will ring through the rest of the salary symphony.

It's been mentioned before: work with concrete goals. What is not concrete is: earning more than last year or more than in your previous job. Concrete goals are a 15 percent higher gross monthly salary, a company car with a minimum book value of £35,000, and a company pension plan commencing 1 January.

Maybe you are asking yourself if a goal is a concrete demand. Sometimes it is, sometimes it isn't. In principle a goal is personal; it does not necessarily need to be declared. It is in your head and perhaps on your cheat sheet. Depending on your negotiation style, personality and relationship with the other party, you could turn a goal into a concrete demand *after* there is an agreement about the gross salary: 'My starting point is a company car. I definitely need it to do my job and to commute. And I am thinking about a car that fits the level of this position, such as a ...'

We have arrived at the third point of this step, determining the order of the negotiable points.

You have a choice of three routes:

1. Firstly based on your 'homework' and the checklists from chapter 4 ('benefits'), make a list and discuss this along with the gross monthly salary. (Obviously you should prepare the list before the meeting.)

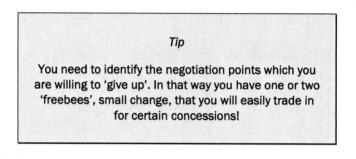

Tip

You need to identify the negotiation points which you are willing to 'give up'. In that way you have one or two 'freebees', small change, that you will easily trade in for certain concessions!

2. The second route is based on the salami technique (refer to chapter 9). You actually only want to talk about the gross salary, so you say. But after there is an agreement on this, you try to get a few benefits.

3. The third way: you say that you have five benefits that you want to discuss, one at a time, without saying what they are. Which order do you choose? Do you have to begin with your most important one and work down the list or the other way around (the climax order)? We advise you to start with the most important (the gross salary) and then to go to the next most important point, perhaps a financial benefit such as a business expense account, or telephone costs. The company car could also be in the second place, depending on the job.

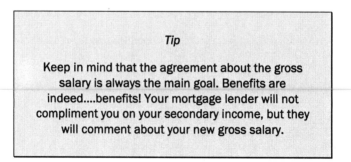

Tip

Keep in mind that the agreement about the gross salary is always the main goal. Benefits are indeed....benefits! Your mortgage lender will not compliment you on your secondary income, but they will comment about your new gross salary.

Step 2. Let the other person speak

You have introduced the meeting and made clear what you want to achieve in terms of salary and benefits. Now you will have to let the other person speak. He will doubtless have worked out all sorts of figures. Perhaps he will now explain what he is able to offer. Perhaps he has already told you there is 'very little leeway'. Or maybe he is smiling as he passes you a piece of paper with his proposal: 'take it or leave it'. But thanks to your preparations you probably have a good idea what the employer may offer. The real negotiations can now begin because both parties have fired off their flares.

Listen well to what your discussion partner says (principle 1) and if necessary make notes!

Of course you can't rule out that your (possible future) boss will come with all kinds of objections and arguments. In chapter 9 we have made a list of a number of the most common arguments along with suitable reactions.

Step 3. Explain your own negotiation points

Don't expect your boss to agree right away with your wishes, no matter how reasonable they are. You will have to have good arguments why you want or deserve this gross salary, why a company car is so necessary and so on.

This step seems more difficult than it is. During this part of the negotiations you can fire off the arguments that you have collected and learned by heart during your preparation! (See chapters 4, 5 and 6. They should give you enough 'evidence' to end the 'battle' with a positive outcome!) For instance you can talk about your 'market value'; you know what an employee with your training and experience is worth. You might present figures that prove that a company car doesn't cost the business anything but actually pays for itself (if it does!). Other objective criteria might include your present salary and benefits (obviously you will need to improve on these), or comparable offers that you have received from other employers.

Tip

Nobody has a perfect memory. So make a 'cheat sheet' with negotiable points and other matter that you want to discuss. A handy trick is to write your points on the left hand side of the sheet and write down notes and agreed on points on the right hand side. Be careful that your interviewer cannot read your notes. (Some people can read 'upside down' very well.) Don't leave the office without your notes.

How many wishes and demands?

You can't dump an unlimited number of demands (or do you call them 'ideas'?) in front of the employer. If you do this, you can expect a negative reaction. The number of wishes that you can discuss depends a lot on their value, your current position, rules, agreements, the organisation's traditions and also the mood and progress of the discussion. A rule of thumb: keep your list to four or five wishes, to which you can add another two, using the salami method discussed in the following chapter.

Step 4. Discuss the possible differences

Perhaps the employer will agree right away with your arguments and your golden ship will quickly sail home. More likely you will have to negotiate on a few or all of the points. How do you move into the next phase when your (prospective) boss has offered you less than you are seeking?

In this phase of the negotiation you can look rather crestfallen and cautiously say, 'I think that we have a problem (then).' And then you fall silent intentionally.

Another assertive approach is to say, 'How can we solve this problem then?' and then you let the other party think about it. Let your opponent take the initiative for a change!

You will notice that during this financial tennis match, the ball will be hit back and forth. And once in a while the ball will go out of bounds. Just as in tennis, the two parties take turns serving.

This phase of the discussion can last a long time. It is handy to keep your head clear by:

- dealing with the points one at a time in order to limit the chance of confusion;
- keep taking notes.

Once in a while you will have to test if what has been offered approaches or meets your goal. (Take a calculator along!)

It is advisable to look at objective criteria when dealing with disagreements. Ask yourself what the motive is for taking a certain position. A model sentence, 'I am not asking for anything unreasonable, so let's look for the points that we both think are reasonable considering the level of this position.'

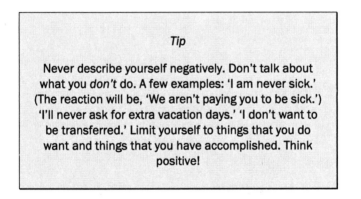

Tip

Never describe yourself negatively. Don't talk about what you *don't* do. A few examples: 'I am never sick.' (The reaction will be, 'We aren't paying you to be sick.') 'I'll never ask for extra vacation days.' 'I don't want to be transferred.' Limit yourself to things that you do want and things that you have accomplished. Think positive!

Step 5. Reach an agreement

Sooner or later you must try reach an agreement. If you are still a long way from attaining your wishes, it is sometimes a good idea to request an adjournment: 'Our ideas are (still) very far apart. I'm not sure we're not going to reach an agreement today. Should we make a new appointment to continue this discussion?'

This strategy has two advantages: you avoid having to repeat arguments that haven't been effective, and you avoid irritation and fatigue. In addition, you give yourself time and space to think of creative solutions.

As the negotiation progresses, keep in mind your shared objectives, in both the short and long-term. 'How can we solve this problem *together*.' Or: 'Let's think of some possible solutions.'

When this process is complete you are approaching closure. But you're not quite there yet.

The results of salary negotiations are often not clear-cut. There are solutions, compromises, 'agreements', suggestions, proposals, ideas, and so on. In addition, there is the phenomenon of selective perception: people only hearing what they want to hear – and selective memory (only remembering what you want to remember!). This means that both parties are not always clear about what has been agreed. Repeat the agreements that have been made (you've written them down) one by one.

The employer will promise to send you a confirmation of the discussion and contract within a few days. If this letter doesn't materialise ask for a written confirmation. It goes without saying that you will compare it with your notes.

Finally, let the other party close the discussion. Your positive and enthusiastic response could be:

♦ 'I'm happy that we have reached an agreement so quickly.'
♦ 'I am looking for to the challenge of this job and I am confident that we will have many pleasant and successful years working together.'
♦ 'We certainly won't regret the agreement we have just reached.'

Betrayed by body language

For some people, salary negotiations are like a game of poker. A good negotiator may be described as having a 'poker face'. He does not show his feelings, or give any indication of his true reactions to a proposal or counter-proposal. There is a total absence of non-verbal signals from the negotiator.

Body language is a two-way street. Be careful of what you reveal by your own body language, and watch your interviewer's body language like a hawk. You need to constantly watch your discussion partner's non-verbal signals (concentrate!) – you would be surprised how much information is hidden in them.

Eye contact

This is your most important signal. Research has shown again and again that when people judge someone as honest, trustworthy and reliable, eye contact counts the most. Pay attention to how you look at the other person, with a cynical gaze, irritated, with a playful or indifferent smile? Or openly and honestly?

Imagine the manager you are negotiating with suddenly asks, 'What gross monthly salary are you thinking of?' You are surprised by this question (you shouldn't be since you have already prepared yourself) and need some time to think. Without realising it you break eye contact. You bend your neck and look at the ceiling. Without making eye contact you say '£3500 a month'. (Your voice sounds doubtful.) Since you didn't look the employer straight in the eye, he will suspect that you just called out anything, fired a loose cannon ball.

Body language

Is the other party sitting comfortably? In other words, is he leaning back with his back on the chair's back? (Men have their legs together while women cross theirs.) Are his arms hanging loosely next to his body? Or are they in his lap (a neutral position). If he has a straight back and his arms are folded over his chest, he is actually saying, 'Come on. I'm listening but you won't convince me easily.' If he crosses his arms during the discussion, he will be less open to your ideas. Or he is finding it difficult to answer your tough questions.

Position

It's been suggested that opponents have the tendency to sit across from each other while allies prefer to sit next to each other. What is your choice? It's best to choose a location for a negotiation that is relaxing. Comfy armchairs and settees, a cosy corner. But be careful that it doesn't get to comfy so that you leave the negotiation as best of friends without having attained your goal.

Emotional undertone

How does your opponent talk? Monotonous or lively? Does it seem like he believes in himself? And what about you? When you don't talk enthusiastically, the other person will draw the conclusion that you don't believe in yourself. And it is your responsibility to make sure your boss thinks otherwise!

> **Tip**
>
> Don't jump to the conclusion that your opponent is smart or is a good negotiator based on a few intelligent remarks. (This is the so called 'halo-effect'.) Base it on more information!

Every day is the right day

When you have not been able to cover all your points in the negotiation, don't give up. In principle you can reopen the negotiations at any moment you want. Why not suggest to your boss that the two of you sit down at the table on the first day of the new quarter. Keep in mind that it takes two to tango – and the other party must 'want to'. And when your boss is open for your arguments, then you may be able to get an element of retrospective compensation (for example, backdated commission) – though it's most unlikely you will get a backdated pay rise!

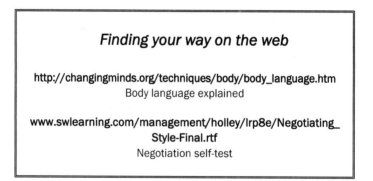

Finding your way on the web

http://changingminds.org/techniques/body/body_language.htm
Body language explained

www.swlearning.com/management/holley/lrp8e/Negotiating_
Style-Final.rtf
Negotiation self-test

9

Less than pleasant negotiations

You now have the tools to get through most negotiations. However, if your boss has you on a short leash and you expect to meet bullying or intransigent resistance to your (reasonable) demands, you will have to be cleverer.

This chapter will teach you how to deal with objections, how to recognise evasive or obstructive negotiation tactics, and how to overcome them. If you are unable to reach a satisfactory agreement, establish a temporary 'working' agreement and call upon reinforcements as and when you are able to do so. We will begin with the objections that the employer will use when your wonderful plans for a fairytale salary crash head on with his totally different vision.

Dismantling the objections

There are objections in every negotiation, raised from time to time by both parties as they respond negatively to a proposal from the other side.

What do you do when you're asked to give a concrete salary proposal (which you do) and the opposing party doesn't agree? First of all, you can ask why a particular part of your proposal is being rejected. Is it clear which part specifically is being turned down? If not, ask. Then you ask a (rather assertive) question such as, 'Why do you have a problem with this?' Little children go through a phase when they want to know 'why' for everything their parents say. Maybe you remember how difficult it is to keep finding suitable answers!

Having asked the question, you patiently wait for the answer. Then you ask a follow up question, 'Is that your only reason?' If the other party says 'yes', then you can begin to disarm this objection by dealing with the reason for the objection. If the answer is 'no', carry on asking questions until you establish all of the reasons for the objection. Deal with each of the reasons in turn until you have (hopefully) either overcome the objection or established a basis for compromise.

> **Tip**
>
> Make the difference between your positions seem
> smaller. When the negotiation is stuck at a difference
> of £400 per month, you can point out to your opponent
> that it is 'only' £100 per week or £20 per day. If
> necessary calculate out that it comes down to a
> measly £2.50 per hour. What are we talking about?

Platitudes and how to unmask them

Perhaps you have heard a number of general unsubstantiated statements designed to deflect your approach. Examples are:

♦ 'These rules are also applied elsewhere (in our sector, in this country, at our other locations, etc.).'
♦ 'I am not authorised to make those decisions.'
♦ 'Shouldn't we talk about the other problems first, before we make a decision?'
♦ 'Let's get some help first from an (internal/external) expert before we hang ourselves.'
♦ 'Your idea/proposal isn't very sound. (But why and how?)'
♦ 'Theoretically this makes sense but in practice we know that it's different.'
♦ 'As I see it, the idea is not financially (legally, etc.) feasible.'
♦ 'Perhaps that's something for the long term.'
♦ 'We shouldn't lose sight of the total cost for our organisation.'

Don't accept this from this adversary and return the ball to his court:

♦ 'Why?' (or 'Why not?')
♦ 'How so?'
♦ 'When can it happen? What conditions does it depend on?'

If you are using these kinds of sentences, your opponent will have to react and come up with logical and reasonable answers. Let him bite into your 'why-questions'! A few other good 'reactions' are:

♦ 'How can we progress this point, then?'
♦ 'What do we/you/I have to do to get my proposal accepted?'
♦ 'How can we get it to work?'
♦ 'Who has to do what in order to...?'

In addition, there are other model sentences to put your opponent in a more positive and creative mood:

♦ 'Let's review all the possibilities.'
♦ 'Where can we get additional industry information in order to establish my final salary?'
♦ 'How would you formulate this clause so that we can both agree?'

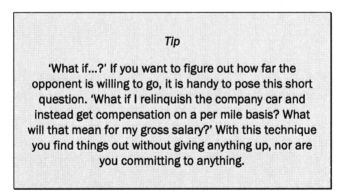

Tip

'What if...?' If you want to figure out how far the opponent is willing to go, it is handy to pose this short question. 'What if I relinquish the company car and instead get compensation on a per mile basis? What will that mean for my gross salary?' With this technique you find things out without giving anything up, nor are you committing to anything.

'Standard procedures!' 'Principles!'

The personnel manager is listening very attentively. He nods in a friendly way to most of your remarks. Your arguments are being accepted – you think. Then he speaks: 'Unfortunately, I can't grant you any of your wishes, however reasonable they are – it's standard procedure.'

What do you do then? First of all, keep in mind that agreements are made by and for people and they are not dictated from heaven. This means that exceptions can always be made. That doesn't mean that *you* will be that exception, but you can ask that one standard rule be changed or bent. Will your request succeed? That depends of course on how much the organisation wants to hire or keep you.

Don't attack the logic or validity of the rule. You will lose this battle (a battle that the other party may have fought before). He will merely point out that everyone is treated the same, that the rules are set down by the head office/board and non-negotiable.

Approach it from a different angle:

♦ 'What happens when that one rule or compensation *isn't* standard for a change?'
♦ 'There must be exceptions within this organisation?' If he answers affirmatively, continue: 'So why can't there be an exception made for me?'
♦ 'Who can I speak to within the organisation who will be able to authorise an exception to this rule? As you will appreciate, this is very important to me'.

'In principle, we can't do that!' says the personnel employee, hoping again to stifle a budding discussion. Maybe you want to get to the heart of the matter this time, knowing that in corporate life principles are often short-lived! Ask suitable questions to allow the other party to distance himself from the offending principle: 'Who established it?' 'With what intention?' 'When was that and what was happening in the organisation at the time?' 'How strict are these principles at the moment?' 'Do they apply to everyone in the organisation including the board of directors?' Your opponent uses an umbrella for his noble principles. Just puncture his shield.

Negotiation tactics

Negotiation territory is full of landmines, which we call tactics. Both parties put them in position and they can also disarm them.

You have to learn to recognise these tactics before you can fight them. Furthermore, you yourself have the option to apply them.

Sanctions

The strongest penalty is that your opponent threatens to end the negotiation, 'As far as I am concerned this negotiation/discussion is finished.' A milder form, 'Naturally, you can always contact our director, Mr Bean. But whether that would be a good move for you career...you'll have to decide that yourself.'

What is important is who has the best cards in his hand? How badly does the organisation want to hire or keep you? And you? Do you need to get a new job in a hurry or do you actually have little need for a going away party at your work?

If there is a threat to curtail the discussion, you could respond with a counter-proposal designed to facilitate early closure, but on your terms:

♦ 'If we reach an agreement now, I'll do everything in my power to reduce my notice to a month by my current employer.'
♦ 'If we can agree with each other now, I am prepared to cancel my holiday.'
♦ 'If we can agree on the contract within a week and its salary, I can give you two extra vacation days a year.'

Delay

This tactic is naturally only used if the other party is in a hurry. Some phrases to use by the employee and employer:

♦ 'We aren't going to reach an agreement today. Let's postpone the negotiations until... (we see some pigs fly).'
♦ 'All the points haven't been worked out yet. It's not possible to draft a definite contract yet.'
♦ 'I want to discuss this with my spouse/lawyer/accountant/tax adviser/counsel, before I come to a definite verdict.'
♦ 'I would like to make these concessions, but first I want to consult with my spouse/lawyer/adviser.'

Exaggeration

Exaggerating or haggling are probably the most well-known negotiation tactics. Both parties name an excessive amount and make extravagant proposals in the hope to end up 'somewhere in the middle'.

The ambush (an unexpected surprise)

This aggressive tactic tries to force a response to a new and unforeseen proposal before the other party has had time to think it through properly. One side comes up with a totally new plan that he has probably taken a lot of time hatching. He magically pulls the rabbit out of the hat. The other party is invited to respond (or, more difficult, to object) there and then. This tactic works well when the other party is in a hurry:

Employer: 'I have a totally new idea, an excellent alternative. I'll offer you a freelance contract that can potentially earn you even more.'

Salami tactic

Salami is a hard garlic sausage that is cut into thin slices. During negotiations, you cut the entire package of demands into pieces and offer them one at a time. The main advantages are that the total wish list is easier to digest and that the opponent will agree to a small demand because the end goal has almost been reached.

Employee: 'I am happy that we have agreed on the gross salary. I want to talk about the fixed expense allowance now.' And after there is an agreement: 'What I almost forgot... my pension premium hasn't been discussed yet. What I had in mind was...'

You can apply the salami tactic in one or more meetings. During the first round, you can reach an agreement about the gross salary. During the following (planned) discussion you bring up the pension insurance or the other parts of the salary such as profit sharing.

A word of warning: if you use this 'sausage method' more than two times during a negotiation, it could become annoying. And that is something you want to avoid.

Making someone feel guilty

Salary negotiator at work:

Employer: 'How can you do this to me, after everything I have done for you lately?'

Employer: 'Why are you making such an impossible demand, when you know that we have rejected all the other candidates for this position?'

Employer: 'You show a lot of understanding for financial matters within our organisation and know that we have invested a lot in you. Why are you making such an exorbitant salary demand now?'

Employee: 'I told my husband that we could absolutely count on a raise. Now you are letting me down. What have I done to deserve this?'

And there are many other ways to play on someone's weaknesses and emotions. Be careful that you don't become a victim!

Bribery

Promise something in the future to encourage acceptance if the immediate proposal:

Employer: 'I can't offer you the desired salary now but in the next round of salary talks I will have more leeway. It goes without saying that when the time comes, you will be considered for a promotion.' (This is known as holding a carrot in front of your nose.)

Employer: 'Unfortunately, I can't offer you that salary but I can promise you participation in our profit-sharing plan.' (How much of this is 'hot air'?)

Making temporary agreements

Who says that you have to come to an agreement in every salary negotiation? Sometimes both parties are just too far apart. Or there can be a genuine timing problem (you run out of it). No agreement can be reached today. Perhaps it is time to draw a line. Do a cost-benefit analysis. What are the costs of making a hasty decision? What would happen if 'the deal' doesn't turn out well? Can you get an idea of the future damage? Sometimes it is a good idea to reject a quick decision. Sometimes it's not.

Another, less dramatic, tactical solution is to settle for a follow-up discussion. Apparently, the parties are not yet ready to make clear, precise agreements on paper but the intention to do so is present. A working agreement is a temporary agreement, which both parties can live with. The players are wise to plan the next round of talks right away.

An example. The employee's salary demand doesn't match what the employer can offer. However, they both want to go further. It's agreed that both parties will think about other compromises. In two weeks, they put their heads together in order to (hopefully) reach an agreement. In accordance with the working agreement, work goes on as usual. The salary remains unchanged until a new agreement has been reached. One thing is okayed: the new salary will be paid retrospectively.

A warning is needed here. A working agreement gives both parties some breathing space. That is the good news. However, the bad news is that a time bomb is ticking away. Until a new agreement is reached, the 'working agreement' will continue to build up resentment and discontent.

Use of evidence

Sometimes your word is enough. But be prepared to be asked for supporting evidence. Take any supporting documentation you think may be appropriate. Think about a salary slip, an article that you have written, a copy of your home page, a photo of in your former employer's magazine, a report (that bears your name or initials), a research paper, proposal, etc.

Well-known mistakes

The other party can be mistaken – and you can be, too. What are the most frequently made mistakes?

1. Your preparation is not up to par. You don't know your options, or what negotiating space you have.
2. You want everything and don't give anything. We have seen that that can lead to unwanted situations, especially in the long term. (The same applies for the stingy, demanding employer.)
3. You try to intimidate the other person. The more outspoken you are the more resistance there will be. Is that what you want?
4. Impatience. Above all, during negotiations, patience is very important. Let the other party have time to 'chew on' your proposals. You will do that as well when your opponent puts a new proposal on the table.
5. Your mood is infectious. If you feel yourself reacting negatively to a particular proposal or tactic, be careful not to show your feelings. Stay calm. Negative emotions work against you.
6. Too much talking and not enough listening is a well-known trap. Turn it around: let the other person talk, while you listen carefully and analyse his intentions thoroughly.
7. Don't be argumentative, and don't contradict. You won't get far with an 'is so-is not' game. You will only irritate the other party.
8. Don't avoid a potential conflict. Negotiations are often carried out with the objective of preventing future problems and conflicts. Therefore, deal with all kinds of difficult matters *now*, so that you have a solid contractual foundation after the negotiations have ended.

9. Don't show any signs of defeat if your opponent has 'beaten' you. Make a record of the circumstances for future reference – and to enable a better outcome next time!

Renegotiating

It is rarely *necessary* to reach an agreement after a single negotiation meeting. It is pleasant and efficient if this is the case, but if it doesn't happen then more rounds will need to be planned. So be it.

When is it not possible to reach a final agreement in one session?

1. The points of view are too far apart. Further discussions are not useful because no new views and arguments are being offered. Fatigue and irritation are starting to take their toll.
2. The 'rank and file' (for instance the personnel department) has to be consulted.
3. Certain questions still remain because (concrete) information is missing.
4. It's possible that you and your information or 'evidence' are not trusted. The other party needs time to check the facts. (Or the other way around.)

If you feel like an agreement is still far away, take out your diary and make a new appointment. Don't let yourself be put under pressure to come to a disadvantageous settlement.

Silences

Many people are afraid of moments of silence during a discussion. They think that a break in the discussion has to be filled with light-hearted chatter. But why don't you make use of the silences? (Maybe your opponent is doing that as well!)

Silence is a negotiation weapon. You can put pressure on the other party. When is it a good idea to keep your mouth shut? First, when your opponent makes a surprise attack. Many think that this needs to be answered amicably with a poker face. As if such a remark had been expected all along! Then there is a quick reply. But has it been well thought out?

A better technique is to organise your thoughts and ideas and say: 'Can I think about that for a moment?' and then keep quiet. You have the right to, don't you? Or do you think that is bad for your image? If you don't find a satisfactory answer after thinking about it, or it is feeling 'sticky', say that it is an interesting point and come back to it later. 'Later' can mean in this discussion or in the following round.

It is also wise to keep your mouth shut if you suspect the other person is lying. Keep quiet and let him continue talking. There is a big chance that he will change his positions and 'adjust' his remark.

Finding your way on the web

www.totalsuccess.co.uk/negotiatingandnegotiationskillstrainin
g.htm
Dealing with tricky negotiators

10

Women on route to a higher salary

In general, women still earn lower salaries than men do, as demonstrated in numerous research reports. It is pretty obvious that women do not have an explicit wish to be paid less than their male colleagues do, and the law clearly forbids unequal pay for the same work. So why the difference? In many cases, this is down simply to negotiation. Women are either less willing to negotiate or less successful at negotiating. One woman: 'I work in the computer sector, a wild west branch. Since this year, I have asked my male colleagues what they are earning. Then you see how big the difference is – and that is mostly due to salary negotiations.'

Whilst the techniques of negotiation are, broadly, universal, there are subtle distinctions between the way that women and men typically approach negotiation, and in the specific skills which each group can bring to bear. In this chapter, we will describe what may be perceived as the weak points of female negotiators and what women can do to overcome them.

Women are being underpaid

Regardless of equal opportunities, numerous international research studies show that women earn less than men for the same work under the same conditions and with the same number of working hours – in spite of the fact that the law forbids discrimination based on gender. There are a number of contributing factors for this discrimination, including, notably, employers' perception of a lack of *career perspective* in women. Just as much to blame is a deficit in simple negotiating skills.

Tip
Be more assertive in explaining to the (future) employer what position you aspire to and why. Do not rely too heavily on soft values such as your enjoyment of teamwork or the working environment. Appear ambitious like the majority of your male co-workers, who present themselves as career tigers.

What women are looking for in a job

According to various sources, women rank job-related issues differently from men, as shown in the chart below. They are more focused on the environment and relationships than on the income.

Women	Workforce
1.Work environment and colleagues	1. Salary
2. Salary	2. Work sphere and colleagues
3. Commuting distance	3. Career chances and training
4. Career chances and training	4. Commuting distance

Sexual manipulation?

There are four possible gender mixes when men and women sit down one-to-one at the negotiating table:

Manager	Employee
1. Man	1. Woman
2. Woman	2. Woman
3. Woman	3. Man
4. Man	4. Man

If there are two 'objective' professionals sitting across from each other, then gender has a limited influence. But what happens if that isn't the case?

In the first scenario where the employee is female and the manager is male, then the woman can make use of her charms and flirt. That may work sometimes but use this strategy with care – it can easily backfire! By the same token, tears can sometimes be very effective in appealing to the more protective male instincts – however, they can also be seen as a sign of weakness!

In the second scenario where a female employee who sits down opposite a female negotiating opponent, the employee needs to be aware that her clothing, jewellery and personal appearance may seen as a threat (jealousy, in simple terms!)

Women are raised differently from men, and are trained for a 'caring' role. That often means that they are polite, considerate and sometimes modest. If you recognise yourself, then you have to stop showing these tendencies when negotiating with a man and attack instead!

Why women are less strong negotiators

Women often take on a weaker position during the game of negotiation. Why is that? Allow a few women to tell you why.

♦ 'We are not businesslike enough, compared to men; we start too low and agree too quickly with the employer's offer. Men will put their own demands on the table sooner than women will.'
♦ 'We are happy with a raise or a promotion and often don't even think about the benefits such as travel costs, health insurance premiums and paid training.'
♦ A project manager at an advertising agency says: 'If I am asked about money, then I get afraid I will come across as arrogant. Or that I will ruin the relationship.'
♦ A lawyer: 'I give up too quickly. Every time that I ask for a pay raise, the employer brings up a number of things that I need to improve and then I back down. Then I often think afterwards: I actually don't agree at all.'

'A little bit more bitchy is allowed sometimes' was the title of a recent article in a Dutch trade union magazine, in which women discussed their feelings about salaries and salary negotiations. What were their concerns?

♦ Women are happy to have got an interesting job (and less concerned with the financial aspect).
♦ Women think of work in terms of enjoyment and belonging – they don't 'need' it so much.
♦ They are afraid of being thought of as cheeky and rude.
♦ They are more prone to suffer from negotiating anxiety. In general, they are more afraid of creating a hostile atmosphere by negotiating.
♦ They are afraid of damage to their reputation or image. They want to keep things 'cosy'.
♦ They are more passive, waiting for the subject of salary to be broached by their bosses, and relying on the principle that a 'good product' will sell itself.
♦ If they are married or in a steady relationship they may not actually *need* their salary. They earn the extras, the icing on the cake. If the

spouse/partner earns well (the classical role pattern!), there is no need to try to get a higher salary.

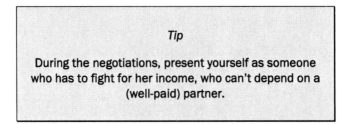

Tip

During the negotiations, present yourself as someone who has to fight for her income, who can't depend on a (well-paid) partner.

◆ Men lobby and put on pressure to get higher up in the organisation and plan ahead for the time when their boss moves on. The king is dead, long live the king!

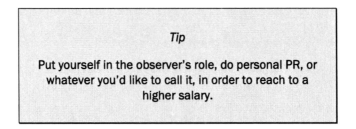

Tip

Put yourself in the observer's role, do personal PR, or whatever you'd like to call it, in order to reach to a higher salary.

◆ Women tend to be more conscious of the balance between work and life, with an increased emphasis on the latter: their children, partner, relationships, etc.
◆ Quite a few women prefer to work part time, and many employers have a problem with that. If it is 'accepted', after some pushing, shoving and supporting – and negotiating – then experienced women find it embarrassing to begin talking about a (higher) salary. They think they have used up all their credit.
◆ Women are easier to charm with non-monetary rewards (titles, pats on the back, recognition.)
◆ Women often take on the care and household responsibilities so that they have less time (and energy) to plan or prepare for a potentially complex negotiation.
◆ Women have a different (and in many respects healthier) view of the world. Non-financial values such as loyalty, recognition, respect, security,

teamwork, integrity, work atmosphere, social relevance and the usefulness of their work are more important than what the work pays. This makes them more vulnerable during negotiations.
♦ Women are less political than men; they spend less time rubbing shoulders with the big bosses, thus they 'hear' less.

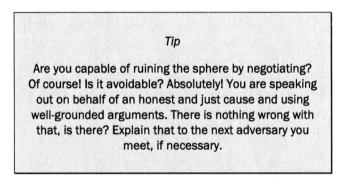

Tip

Are you capable of ruining the sphere by negotiating? Of course! Is it avoidable? Absolutely! You are speaking out on behalf of an honest and just cause and using well-grounded arguments. There is nothing wrong with that, is there? Explain that to the next adversary you meet, if necessary.

Being brushed off

Which arguments will tempt women? What do they 'fall' for? We name a few examples in random order:

♦ They attach more value to the content of the work than on the money. Bosses can easily take advantage of the argument 'money can't buy happiness'. For example by dryly remarking that 'our people aren't motivated by money'. Alternatively: 'If you really want to earn a lot then you have to get into the IT sector, the stock exchange or start selling coke.' Don't let yourself be misled by these kinds of remarks!
♦ Women are more sensitive than men are when it comes to applying emotional tactics. In chapter 9, we explained which ones could be fired at you and how to defend against them. Example: the employer has just paid your additional training costs and now you want to punish him again financially. (Sigh, moan.) In this case, they want you to feel guilty.
♦ The negotiator says that no top salaries can be granted and switches the conversation smartly to the poor conditions elsewhere such as terrible commuting or a 'female-unfriendly' environment (changing the focus of the conversation to areas in which the employer has a strong personal interest).

If you are getting 'nowhere' during the negotiation, you can make use of the following arguments: 'I have been working in this department for five years now, my performance is well known, what can you do for me to keep me?' Or: 'How do you suggest that we solve my problem?' 'I am not asking for more, more, more but what I deserve based on what I have done for this company.'

Tip

It is no bad thing to tell your boss how interesting you think the work is, how much benefit it has for society, how important it is for yourself. But that is separate from the money that you need to earn every month.

Doing more certainly helps!

If you work part-time, it doesn't have to mean that the employer receives that exact proportion of your creativity, attention and energy for his pennies. Do more than is expected in your employment contract. Here are a few examples of how you can do more for the organisation:

- Make yourself available for overtime.
- Offer to help others with work problems or personal situations.
- Organise pub nights and other social activities.
- Make suggestions regarding improvements for procedures, administration, job descriptions and the like.
- Don't use any company time for personal business (since that is 'time theft'.)
- Voluntarily organise a study trip.
- Don't complain about temporary inconveniences.

Less often or not now

If you are tired from negotiating (not again!), then do it less often but better! For instance, you can propose now what periodic raises (gross salary and benefits) you want in the coming years. Get any agreement written down.

If you happen to have a domestic crisis (perhaps with your children) right before a negotiation, then your head won't be thinking about the negotiation. So put the negotiation off.

Warnings!

Negotiating is not a matter of life or death. Think about that when your nerves are tying a knot in your stomach. Maybe these words will calm you. During negotiations you will seldom reach the best agreement, but may nevertheless achieve the optimal outcome, considering the circumstances.

If you come out of the negotiation with much less than you had hoped, you can throw all kinds of blame at yourself, but that won't help the situation. Be positive and constructive. Analyse what went wrong so that you can do better next time. Besides, it could be that there simply wasn't any more you could have done since the bottom of the employer's pork barrel had been reached! Don't see the setback as a personal rejection or defeat.

Finding your way on the web

www.whatsheearns.co.uk
Information on pay, salaries and wages for women

www.iea.org.uk/record.jsp?type=release&ID=149
Institute of Economic Affairs article on the gender pay gap

11

Winding it all up

We have followed the negotiation process more or less chronologically. In this last chapter, we only have to dot the 'i's and cross the 't's.

We recommend, as previously stated, that everything you agree is confirmed in writing. This has a number of obvious advantages, particularly when it comes to your next salary review.

*Sometimes it's necessary for **you** to provide the written confirmation yourself, but it is usually your employer's responsibility. Where you enter into a new contract of employment, the results of your salary negotiations will normally be found either in the body of the contract or in its appendixes.*

The employment contract

If you are taking on a new position or a new job, make sure that everything you have agreed is included in an employment contract. It can be difficult to talk with a (future) boss who has a memory problem! When your employer tries to avoid written confirmation of your agreements, you will need convince him that the record will be useful for both parties. If he questions your trust, deal with this as follows:

Employer: 'Why do we have to write it down? Don't you trust me?'

Employee: 'It's never crossed my mind to not trust you! Otherwise we wouldn't be sitting here together'

What should and shouldn't be put in the contract? That depends on a number of things. You are already 'protected' by employment law. Companies and organisations often have standard contracts that, whether or not adapted, can be used. Many accountants and lawyers also have these readily available.

Ask yourself a few critical questions before you sign the contract:

1. Is this contract in my favour?
2. What is not in the contract that I think should be?
3. What possible hidden dangers are there in the offered contract? (Play the devil's advocate – imagine you are a boss trying to use the contract to the employee's disadvantage!)

> **Tip**
>
> **A signed contract is not necessarily permanent. The contract, or parts of it, are always 'discussable' – and re-negotiating a contract (or changing or adding to it) is sometimes essential, for example, when tasks and responsibilities have changed drastically.**

Title and job description

Does the final contract also include your suggested title and your job description? Perhaps you feel you can go in, blindly trusting your (new) boss – perhaps it doesn't matter to you so much what title he chooses. However, you need to think ahead. His successor may have a different vision of your job responsibilities and salary. One glance at your employment contract and he may decide to give you other tasks, which may have a direct impact on your earning potential. And it's not just your salary which may be under threat from the replacement boss – you may also find yourself having to say goodbye to your beautiful and comfortable office and other associated status symbols. In addition, when you leave this employer, you are worth more to your new employer if you have a prestigious title on your business card.

Pay particular attention to the clauses spelling out who you have to *report to*. This is usually your direct boss.

This reveals two things:

1. It defines the status of your position, as one step below the level of the person you report to (your boss).
2. It can prevent your having to report to someone other than the person you understood would be your boss.

It can also indicate that you are a promising star in the night sky, reporting directly to the higher gods!

We hope that you are not only promising but that you can also fulfil your promises.

A temporary contract (limited duration)

More and more employers are offering new employees (from high to low) a short-term agreement, instead of a permanent contract. There are clear reasons for this:

♦ The initial temporary contract may be regarded as a probationary arrangement. One gets to know an employee in day-to-day real situations – their professional qualities, as well as social, leadership, commercial and other capacities are revealed.
♦ It is a way to test the self-confidence of the future employee. A person who doesn't believe in himself may well refuse to sign such a contract. Maybe he thinks that he can't 'prove' his worth in the initial contract period. (Trust in the employer may also be absent.)
♦ Employment law can make it costly for employers to let employees go. A temporary contract ends automatically.
♦ The employer can hedge his bets when it's difficult to predict what the future will bring. (How will the economy develop in the next couple of years? And company sales? Will the current subsidy be extended?)

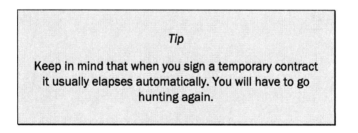

Tip

Keep in mind that when you sign a temporary contract it usually elapses automatically. You will have to go hunting again.

Most temporary employment contracts last for six to twelve months. However, it is possible to have a contract for a specific project. For instance, this (sometimes vaguely described) project could last for two to five years, or three months. A probationary period can included in the temporary contract but this is not always the case. During the probationary period, both parties can dissolve the contract immediately without a reason. If there isn't a probationary period, then the work continues for the entire contract period (or, if the work ceases before the end of the period, the employer remains liable to pay the agreed salary for the full period).

Tip

It's advisable not to make any verbal agreements on top of the employment contract. These can be forgotten or misinterpreted – and if your boss falls under the proverbial bus, his successor, however trustworthy, will have no record to go by.

Legal help?

Is it necessary to call on the help of a lawyer for your employment contract? Sometimes, since preventing a problem is better than trying to solve it after the fact. And probably cheaper! When you are presented with a contract with unusual points or strange clauses or a rather broadly written non-competition clause, it is a good idea to seek a lawyer's advice.

Always ask for time to study the contract before you sign it. Don't be afraid. A handy sentence to use: 'I would like to take the time to read the contract. Maybe I need to ask for some advice about a few details. Is it agreeable if I call you in five days? Then we can make any changes or adjustments over the phone. Could we agree to that?'

In the meantime, you can always get in contact with a lawyer.

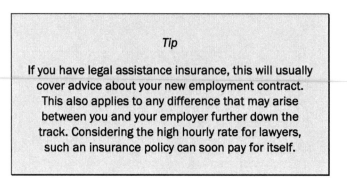

Tip

If you have legal assistance insurance, this will usually cover advice about your new employment contract. This also applies to any difference that may arise between you and your employer further down the track. Considering the high hourly rate for lawyers, such an insurance policy can soon pay for itself.

Non-competition clause

Companies are often fearful that an employee will quit and then start working for a competitor, or start his own competing business. Many employers are sad when they see all their years of hard won knowledge disappearing out of the door – together with several clients and/or colleagues. In this respect, employers are justified in seeking to protect themselves. This is covered by the non-competition clause(s) in the employment contract.

Every firm has the right to protect its interests, but how long should the restrictions on leaving employees last? A worker has the freedom to choose the work he wants – unless he has signed a non-competition clause that disallows that. This presents a dilemma. Happily, the terms in the clause can be negotiated.

It is not always easy for the ex-employer to enforce a non-competition clause. The judge – if it comes to that – has to consider the interests of two parties: the employer and the employee. Points that are considered include:

♦   Does the employee pose a material or specific threat to the ex-employer (for example, in relation to a new technology)?

♦   Is the employee being prevented from working (for example by preventing him from practising the profession he has been schooled for)?

The judge has the power to shorten the period or terms of reference of the non-competition clause or dismiss it all together.

The duration of the clause can vary, but is usually for one year. During this time the employee may be prevented from taking specific types of employment (within particular industries, or working for specific companies) and the embargo may preclude consulting or part-time work as well as full-time employment. Sometimes a 'price tag' may be attached to the clause, resulting in a fine in the event of breach – for example £1000 per day – and that adds up quickly.

The non-competition clause is seldom part of the salary negotiation. After reaching a verbal agreement, the employee will find the clause in the offered contract. Since it is assumed that you will agree with all the clauses and amounts, are you allowed to refuse to sign the contract because of the non-competition clause? Of course! You can ask the employer to take the clause out, to ease the terms, decrease the fine, etc. The boss can be stubborn. What do you do then? How badly do you want the job and how badly does the employer want you?

If you have any doubts about the severity of the non-competition clause, get the advice of a lawyer.

How can you avoid the non-competition clause?

Imagine that you definitely don't want a non-competition clause in the contract. What do you do then?

♦ Demand that it is taken out of the contract. As a job applicant or employee, you must obviously be in a strong position to take this line!

♦ Agree, but quantify the value of the clause, and ask for an equivalent benefit (perhaps monetary). Obviously you will need to agree the 'value' and the chosen amount must be explicitly noted in the contract. In other words, you want to see money in exchange for the clause.

♦ Soften your demands: accept the clause but only during the duration of the contract and not for the period afterwards. Then it is basically not a non-competition clause any more.

♦ Decrease the period of time the clause is valid. For instance, if the duration was a year after leaving the company, propose that it be three to six months.

♦ A clause can also be limited to a geographic area. So change a national ban to a ban in London and a radius of 20 miles around this city.

♦ The alternative is to narrow down the businesses or jobs covered by the clause.

♦ The last remedy: 'See you in court.' Let the judge rule on the disputed clause. (Potentially an expensive option!)

Relationship clause

The non-competition clause ascertains that in a number of circumstances your employer's competitor cannot employ you. A relationship clause goes one step further. It prevents you from 'stealing', or dealing with, your old boss' clients. This can be very restrictive. The same negotiation principles apply as for the non-competition clause – try to reduce the period, or to narrow down the definition of companies you cannot deal with. If you have to sign an employment contract with this kind of clause, you would be well advised to try to have it omitted by negotiation – trade something in!

Finding your way on the web

**www.adviceguide.org.uk/index/life/employment/contracts_of
_employment**
Citizens Advice Bureau on employment contracts

www.wikipedia.org
Explanations of employment contracts

**www.direct.gov.uk/en/Employment/Employees/EmploymentC
ontractsAndConditions/DG_10027905**
Government advice on employment contracts

Epilogue

You now have all the tools to navigate through your next salary negotiation. Will you also 'win'? We have indicated that if you are the only winner coming out of the negotiation, it is not a good situation. What is important is that both parties win and that they find it pleasant and advantageous to work together for many years to come. A truly win-win situation.

You hold the keys to keep having better negotiations: preparation, practice and being critical towards yourself. When you grab hold of every chance to train (instead of avoiding it), your skills will improve immensely.

Lots of luck!

Useful Websites

(as listed throughout the book)

www.monster.co.uk
Tips about salaries and incomes

www.jobcentreplus.gov.uk
Jobsearch and benefits advice

www.nomisweb.co.uk
Labour market information

www.statistics.gov.uk/STATBASE/Product.asp?vlink=550
Labour market statistics

www.prospects.ac.uk/cms/ShowPage/Home_page/Labour_market_information/p!efeXak
Labour market information for graduates

www.thesalaryindicator.co.uk
To calculate net pay

www.hmrc.gov.uk/nmw
National minimum wage

www.wageindicator.org
www.payscale.com/resources.aspx?nc=lp_calculator_united kingdom01
www.reed.co.uk/CareerTools/SalaryCalculator.aspx
Payscale guidelines

www.employeebenefits.co.uk
Latest developments and regulations governing employee benefits

www.ashworthblack.co.uk
Advisors on alternative remuneration structures, bonus schemes and employee benefits

www.hmrc.gov.uk/paye/exb-intro-basics.htm
Guide to the tax implications of different kinds of benefits

http://www.hmrc.gov.uk/guidance/relocation.htm
HMRC advice on relocation

http://content.monster.co.uk/section323.asp
Job interview advice

www.cipd.co.uk/subjects/perfmangmt/appfdbck/perfapp.htm
Chartered Institute of Personnel and Development advice on
appraisals

www.admin-ezine.com/performance_appraisals_toc.htm
An ezine review of appraisal strategies for employees

www.i-resign.com/UK/resigning/
Advice on how to quit or resign

http://content.monster.co.uk/15196_en-GB_p1.asp
Advice on preparing for interviews

www.bspcn.com/2007/08/24/10-killer-job-interview-
questions-and-answers/
Ten more killer questions

http://changingminds.org/techniques/body/body_language.htm
Body language explained

www.swlearning.com/management/holley/lrp8e/Negotiating_
Style-Final.rtf
Negotiation self-test

www.totalsuccess.co.uk/negotiatingandnegotiationskillstrainin
g.htm
Dealing with tricky negotiators

www.whatsheearns.co.uk
Information on pay, salaries and wages for women

www.iea.org.uk/record.jsp?type=release&ID=149
Institute of Economic Affairs article on the gender pay gap

**www.adviceguide.org.uk/index/life/employment/contracts_of
_employment**
Citizens Advice Bureau on employment contracts

www.wikipedia.org
Explanations of employment contracts

**www.direct.gov.uk/en/Employment/Employees/EmploymentC
ontractsAndConditions/DG_10027905**
Government advice on employment contracts

Index